contents
TABLE OF CONTENTS

v **FOREWORD**
Lee S. Shulman, President, The Carnegie Foundation for the Advancement of Teaching

1 **INTRODUCTION**
Ethics and Aspiration in the Scholarship of Teaching and Learning
Pat Hutchings, Vice President, The Carnegie Foundation for the Advancement of Teaching

19 **CASE 1**
The Ethics of Comparison: A Statistician Wrestles with the Orthodoxy of a Control Group
John P. Holcomb Jr., Mathematics, Cleveland State University
- 22 **COMMENTARY 1** Roberto L. Corrada, Law, University of Denver College of Law
- 23 **COMMENTARY 2** Joan B. Garfield, Educational Psychology, University of Minnesota
- 25 **COMMENTARY 3** Caroline Hodges Persell, Sociology, New York University

27 **CASE 2**
Using Student Work as Evidence
David Takacs, Environmental Humanities, California State University, Monterey Bay
- 31 **COMMENTARY 1** Amy Driscoll, Director, Teaching, Learning, and Assessment, California State University, Monterey Bay
- 32 **COMMENTARY 2** Kevin Miller, Student, California State University, Monterey Bay
- 33 **COMMENTARY 3** Cynthia Scheinberg, English, Mills College

35 **CASE 3**
Refining Questions and Renegotiating Consent
Suzanne Burgoyne, Theatre, University of Missouri–Columbia
- 39 **COMMENTARY 1** Richard Gale, Theatre Arts and Interdisciplinary Studies, Hutchins School of Liberal Studies, Sonoma State University
- 40 **COMMENTARY 2** Peter J. Markie, Philosophy, University of Missouri–Columbia
- 43 **COMMENTARY 3** Helen A. Neville, Educational Psychology and Afro-American Studies and Research Program, University of Illinois at Urbana–Champaign

47 **CASE 4**
Balancing Pedagogic Needs with the Needs of a Classroom Experiment
Charles McDowell, Computer Science, University of California, Santa Cruz
- 50 **COMMENTARY 1** Peter Alexander, Mathematics, Heritage College
- 51 **COMMENTARY 2** Heather E. Bullock, Psychology, University of California, Santa Cruz
- 52 **COMMENTARY 3** Eileen M. Tanner, Director, Center for Teaching Excellence, University of California, Santa Cruz

55 **CASE 5**
Too Close for Comfort and/or Validity?
Tomás Galguera, Education, Mills College
- 60 **COMMENTARY 1** Camille Calica, Teacher, Shepherd Elementary School, Hayward, California
- 60 **COMMENTARY 2** David M. Donahue, Education, Mills College
- 62 **COMMENTARY 3** Judith Haymore Sandholtz, Education, University of California, Riverside

TABLE OF CONTENTS

65   **CASE 6**
From Private to Public Classrooms: "Inadequate" Student Texts in the Scholarship of Teaching and Learning
James E. Seitz, English, University of Pittsburgh
- 69   **COMMENTARY 1**   Christie Raney, Student, English and Education, University of Pittsburgh
- 69   **COMMENTARY 2**   Mariolina Rizzi Salvatori, English, University of Pittsburgh
- 71   **COMMENTARY 3**   Annette Seitz, Resident Fellow, Institute for Learning, Learning Research and Development Center, University of Pittsburgh

75   **CASE 7**
Going Public with Students' Work: The Movie
Sherry Linkon, English and American Studies, Youngstown State University
- 78   **COMMENTARY 1**   Randy Bass, English and American Studies, Georgetown University
- 79   **COMMENTARY 2**   Thomas Hatch, Senior Scholar, The Carnegie Foundation for the Advancement of Teaching
- 81   **COMMENTARY 3**   John Stern, Videographer and President, West Peak Media, Inc.

85   **QUESTIONS TO SHAPE PRACTICE**

87   **ANNOTATED BIBLIOGRAPHY**
Research Ethics and the Scholarship of Teaching and Learning
James Bequette, Research Assistant, The Carnegie Foundation for the Advancement of Teaching
Chris Bjork, Education, Vassar College

97   **BIOGRAPHICAL NOTES**

Ethics of Inquiry

Issues in the Scholarship of Teaching and Learning

Pat Hutchings, Editor
*The Carnegie Foundation
for the Advancement of Teaching*

A Publication of
**The Carnegie Foundation for
The Advancement of Teaching**

Acknowledgments

Many have contributed to this effort and I want to thank them, starting with my colleagues here at the Carnegie Foundation. Senior Scholars Mary Huber and Tom Hatch both read sections of the manuscript at an early stage and provided invaluable feedback. Gay Clyburn, director of communications and information, along with her staff and freelancers, helped move the project from inspiration to finished product. Megan Gutelius and others in the Carnegie Information Center helped with background research, and research assistants James Bequette and Chris Bjork put together the extensive Annotated Bibliography. Barbara Cambridge, our colleague at the American Association for Higher Education who provides leadership for work on CASTL campuses, has been a consistent voice for making students active agents and collaborators in the scholarship of teaching and learning—a theme that runs through this volume. And Carnegie President Lee Shulman has supplied not only a thoughtful Foreword but also the intellectual leadership for Carnegie's work on the scholarship of teaching and learning.

Acknowledgments are due, as well, to the many individuals and groups participating in the Carnegie Academy for the Scholarship of Teaching and Learning. It's not possible to identify their contributions one by one, but in various ways, and over several years, their hard questions, good counsel, and "reality checks" have directly shaped this volume.

Finally, I want especially to thank the seven case authors and their respondents (faculty, students, and others) for sharing their experiences and perspectives with such candor and thoughtfulness. The commitment they demonstrate to understanding and improving student learning is what the scholarship of teaching and learning is all about.

—Pat Hutchings

Book design by Leap O Faith Design. Cover design by Amanda Yu. Copyediting by Laurie Milford. Dictionary entries on the cover are used by permission. From *Webster's Third New International® Dictionary, Unabridged*© 1993 by Merriam-Webster, Incorporated.

© 2002 The Carnegie Foundation for the Advancement of Teaching.
All rights reserved. Printed in the United States of America.

Library of Congress Cataloging-in-Publication Data

Ethics of inquiry : issues in the scholarship of teaching and learning / edited by Pat Hutchings.
    p. cm.
Includes bibliographical references.
 ISBN 0-931050-70-7 (pbk. : alk. paper)
 1. College teachers—Professional ethics—United States—Case studies. 2. College teaching—Moral and ethical aspects—United States—Case studies. I. Title: Issues in the scholarship of teaching and learning. II. Hutchings, Pat.
 LB1779 .E755 2002
  378.1'2—dc21
                       2002005471

For more information about The Carnegie Foundation for the Advancement of Teaching, please consult our Web site: **www.carnegiefoundation.org**.

Additional copies of this publication are available from:

    Carnegie Publications
    The Carnegie Foundation for the Advancement of Teaching
    555 Middlefield Road
    Menlo Park, California 94025
    Phone 650/566-5128
    Fax 650/326-0278

Single copies are $27, plus shipping. For information on bulk orders, contact Carnegie Publications.

FOREWORD

A few months ago, I participated in a site visit with a Carnegie Foundation team to a prominent school of engineering. When we asked both students and faculty the rather straightforward question, "What is an engineer?" we generally heard some version of the following reply: "An engineer uses mathematics and sciences to design and create things—products, artifacts—that make a difference in the world and help people to live in it." Teachers and students alike emphasized the essentially practical character of engineering as a profession that employs thought in the interests of design.

Messing with the World

A number of the respondents did not stop there, however. They went on to emphasize that once you messed with the world, you became responsible for your designs, both as they were used and also when they were no longer useful. Designed products are visible, tangible, useful, intrusive, helpful, dangerous, beautiful, ugly, and potentially eternal. Therefore, they argued, engineers should be responsible not only for what they design, but also for the life cycle of their products, for their ultimate fates as well as their immediate utilities. I was deeply impressed by their sensitivity to the connections between the practical and the ethical. As soon as you mess with the world, you take on responsibility for what you've done.

This is a point that Aristotle understood well. For him, ethics was the central focus of the practical, as distinct from the theoretical. Theoretical inquiries lead to new ideas; practical reason leads to action that makes a difference in the world. Practical work necessarily entails ethical problems—trade-offs between alternate paths, judging the prudence of one's actions. And so it is with the scholarship of teaching and learning.

The Ethics of Teaching and Scholarship

What, after all, could be more quintessentially practical than that distinctly human activity, teaching? Indeed, the practical end of teaching is changing minds, and in changing minds to help learners to understand and perform, use and enjoy, interact and relate differently than they might have otherwise. To put it another way, teaching is an intentional, designed act undertaken to influence the minds of others, and to change the world in an intensely intimate, socially responsible manner.

Such work brings with it inexorable responsibilities. Having engaged students through an act of instruction, the teacher becomes at least partially responsible for its efficacy. It is unimaginable that a teacher could teach with no concern for whether students had learned, how well they had learned, or whether their learning was appropriate to the field.

And what about scholarship? To many folks, the juxtaposition of "scholarship" and "practical" seems an oxymoron, as bizarre a conjunction as "research" and "teaching." Research has, after all, been viewed as the ultimate theoretical pursuit, with objectivity, anonymity, and *dis*engagement as its hallmarks. But

Foreword

the message of this volume is that research, especially when undertaken in the pursuit of teaching and learning, is eminently practical in the richest sense of the word. As such, acts of scholarship focused on one's teaching and the quality of learning for one's students are *practical* acts, with inevitable consequences for those involved. In short, it should not surprise us that both teaching and the scholarship of teaching are strategic sites for encountering an array of ethical challenges.

Making It Public … and Generalizable

A philosopher (it may have been Max Black) once observed that philosophy begins in wonder and ends in algebra. It might similarly be observed that scholarship necessarily begins in private and ends in public. Teaching, while conducted in the public forum of a classroom, is typically a clandestine act. The scholarship of teaching makes the private public and the clandestine observable. Once the work of teaching is public, new ethical dilemmas arise.

A number of years ago, Judy Shulman published an article titled "Now You See Them, Now You Don't: Anonymity Versus Visibility in Case Studies of Teachers" *(Educational Researcher,* 1990, 19(5), 11–15). The tradition of educational research was that teachers were invisible and anonymous. They were studied by others. They were not individuals; they were clusters of behaviors or cognitions or personality variables. They were the ultimate research subjects, devoid of identity or agency. And if the teachers were subordinated to "instructional treatments," then what could be said of the students? They were even further submerged, captured in average test scores, in percentages of males and females, or in categories of socioeconomic status.

Judy's work was central to a somewhat Copernican revolution in the study of teaching, especially with regard to the role of teachers. She worked with teachers to become scholars of their own practice, to document their work and to write it up in narrative and analytic cases of teaching and learning. As in medicine, these were "problem" or "dilemma" driven cases, constructed around unexpected difficulties that the teachers had encountered, coped with, analyzed, reflected upon, and were now prepared to share. As those cases moved from private stories to published case studies, a set of new challenges, including ethical ones, arose.

Like many of the best examples of the scholarship of teaching and learning, the cases written by teachers working with Judy included rich particulars about context—detailed renderings of the school, the students, the curriculum, and the situations in which the key episodes of the case take place. These details are essential for others seeking to generalize from the cases. When I read a case study (or, for that matter, the report of an experiment or a survey), I need always to ask, What is this a case of? How similar are the circumstances under which this study was conducted to the situation to which I might wish to generalize its findings? Is this work relevant to me and my circumstances? Without substantial detail, I cannot ask these all-important questions about the work's contribution to the scholarship of teaching and learning.

But the same details that allow for generalizability also make cases potentially embarrassing to both protagonist and setting, since they often examine a collision between design and chance. The cases that Judy worked to develop were personally authored, so the teachers could take responsibility for the practices they were reporting. Yet when an authored, fully rendered case is made public, the veil of anonymity and privacy that protected the "subjects" is lifted. They are no longer safe from observation, from criticism, from exposure.

Judy and the teachers with whom she worked thus confronted ethical dilemmas very like those represented in this volume. If the scholarship of teaching does not include rich contextual detail, it may lose much of its value for others who might study and learn from the work. At the same time, every detail threatens to expose other teachers, students, and programs to uninvited scrutiny. If even the name of the teacher-author is made public, the wall of confidentiality is breached. Is that ethical? Can a teacher doing research on her own practice publish cases and other forms of scholarly work analyzing that practice if the details of the work (including its authorship) subject others to unwanted visibility? And even if permission has been granted by those immediately involved, can they possibly anticipate the many ways in which the work might be studied, interpreted, used, and disseminated?

The issues of visibility and anonymity are but one facet of the growing set of questions around the ethics of a scholarship of teaching and learning. The only way to avoid confronting such ethical dilemmas in professional work would be to stop acting entirely. And that would itself be unethical.

An Example from Medical Practice

We read the same story in the news at least once a year. In one version, a passenger on a cross-country airline experiences severe heart pain and the cabin attendant asks if there is a physician on board. A physician comes forward and attempts to assist the patient, but after several interventions the patient dies. Subsequently, the family of the deceased sues the airline and the physician, the latter for malpractice. Had the physician remained in her seat and withheld her professional service, she would have been held harmless, no questions asked.

In the other version of the story, an auto accident leaves several people badly injured by the roadside. A physician drives by and decides not to stop and render medical assistance for fear that he will be held responsible for any care he delivers. He is later criticized for inaction, for an unwillingness to act professionally. Once a person or a community takes on the mantle of a profession, every act is potentially permeated with ethical questions. This is not, as Pat Hutchings argues in the Introduction, a symptom of trouble, but a sure sign of maturity.

The Pedagogical Imperative

Much of Carnegie's work is organized around the scholarship of teaching and learning. This concept of a scholarship of teaching and learning not only describes a type of research that the Foundation conducts and supports. It is also a concept of moral action, aimed at cultural change. The scholarship of teaching and learning rests, that is, on a moral claim that I will call the "pedagogical imperative." We argue that an educator can teach with integrity only if an effort is made to examine the impact of his or her work on the students. The "pedagogical imperative" includes the obligation to inquire into the consequences of one's work with students. This is an obligation that devolves on individual faculty members, on programs, on institutions, and even on disciplinary communities.

FOREWORD

Inherent in this vision is the idea of teacher as steward of his or her field of study. As such, those of us who teach are responsible for the integrity of that field as it is understood by others. We are responsible for what is learned, how it is learned, what value it has for students, and for our own learning through practice in ways that make us more effective in fostering important forms of learning for all students. The scholarship of teaching and learning is an instrument and a disposition for fulfilling that stewardship and sustaining that quest for integrity. But, as this volume illustrates, the very act of such scholarship introduces a new layer of responsibilities, a novel universe of ethical questions. Pat Hutchings, the Carnegie Scholars, and all others who contributed to this volume as case writers and as commentators have offered their contributions to the advancement of the scholarship of teaching.

Scholars of teaching and learning are prepared to mess with the world even more boldly than their colleagues who are satisfied to teach well and leave it at that. They mess with their students' minds and hearts as they instruct, and then they mess again as they examine the quality of those practices and ask how they could have been even more effective. Scholars of teaching and learning are prepared to confront the ethical as well as the intellectual and pedagogical challenges of their work. They are not prepared to be drive-by educators. They insist on stopping at the scene to see what more they can do.

—*Lee S. Shulman*
*President, The Carnegie Foundation
for the Advancement of Teaching
Spring 2002*

INTRODUCTION

Ethics and Aspiration in the Scholarship of Teaching and Learning

Pat Hutchings
Vice President
The Carnegie Foundation for the Advancement of Teaching

For the past five years, The Carnegie Foundation for the Advancement of Teaching has been undertaking a national effort to develop the scholarship of teaching and learning. This work has a history in most academic fields—and sometimes a cadre of people who are specialists in it (Huber and Morreale, 2002). But for many faculty the scholarship of teaching and learning is new terrain. They may, for instance, be excellent teachers, but typically they have not treated their classrooms as sites for systematic inquiry; framing their own teaching problems as questions of broader scholarly significance entails a real shift of perspective (Bass, 1999). Similarly, faculty come to the scholarship of teaching and learning as experts in their fields, but they're often uncertain how to use the field's concepts and methods to explore teaching and learning. The very idea of documenting and sharing the work of teaching and learning—a core principle of the scholarship of teaching and learning—is new to most faculty.

Not surprisingly in all this novelty, the scholarship of teaching and learning also presents ethical issues that are new to many faculty. Is it necessary to have permission to use excerpts from student papers, or data from their exams, in my scholarship of teaching and learning? If so, what kind of permission is appropriate, and how should it be secured? Should I (must I?) submit my project design to the campus Institutional Review Board (IRB), which monitors work with human subjects? *Are* students human subjects? Do I need their informed consent to begin my work? To publish it? The scholarship of teaching and learning calls on us to "make teaching community property" (Lee Shulman's phrase), but what are the appropriate boundaries between public and private? Who owns what goes on in the classroom? Who benefits, and who is at risk, when the complex dynamics of teaching and learning are documented and publicly represented?

As one of the leaders of Carnegie's program on the scholarship of teaching and learning (the Carnegie Academy for the Scholarship of Teaching and Learning—or CASTL, as we call it), I've heard these questions in many variations, and I've heard them with greater frequency over the past few years. I hear them from the 114 faculty, from some twenty fields, who have been selected as fellows with CASTL's center for advanced study, and I hear them on campuses (some 200 now) participating in the program. Ethical issues were the topic of a discussion at a session on the scholarship of teaching and learning I attended at the American Sociological Association meeting in summer 2001, and at a special forum at the Modern Language Association meeting in December 2001. Questions about ethics turned up recently, as well, in discussion on a national listserv of faculty developers, with participants

INTRODUCTION

asking one another for advice about appropriate campus policies and processes. In short, it seems safe to say that ethical issues raised by the scholarship of teaching and learning are increasingly in the air. This volume aims to address the emerging need to understand and deal with such issues—by mapping themes, clarifying contexts, and providing examples.

At the same time, the materials gathered here, including this introductory essay, make it clear that ethical issues often do not lend themselves to definite answers, that there can be no one-size-fits-all rules. Like other aspects of the scholarship of teaching and learning, its ethical dimensions are shaped by discipline, context, and purpose. What's needed most is not, then, a set of rules but a process of reflection, self-questioning, and discussion. As noted in the *Handbook on Ethical Issues in Anthropology*, a publication of the American Anthropological Association, it's difficult to formulate "a code specific enough to use as a mechanism of social control," but ethical principles and the process of devising them can be "a way of reflecting upon our own practices and attempting to improve them" (Cassell and Jacobs, 1987: 1). In short, the way a field frames and thinks about ethical issues is a window into its character

> **The Carnegie Academy for the Scholarship of Teaching and Learning (CASTL)**
>
> The Carnegie Academy for the Scholarship of Teaching and Learning supports the scholarship of teaching in colleges and universities, as well as in K–12 settings. The program seeks to make teaching public, subject to critical evaluation, and usable by others in ways that will foster significant, long-lasting learning for all students, enhance the practice and profession of teaching, and bring to faculty members' work as teachers the recognition and stature afforded to other forms of scholarly work.
>
> The higher education program has three components. *The Carnegie Scholars Program*, launched in 1998, supports the work of faculty members from across the spectrum of disciplines who are exploring questions about the teaching and learning of their fields. The program operates on the model of an advanced study center, aiming to advance work that has broad significance and that others can build on. *The Teaching Academy Campus Program* works with campuses seeking to create a culture in which the scholarship of teaching and learning can flourish. The American Association for Higher Education (AAHE) coordinates this program, working with campuses of all types. CASTL's *work with scholarly and professional societies* supports the development of new language, standards, vehicles, and occasions for conducting and exchanging the scholarship of teaching and learning.

(the pun is deliberate)—that is, how it thinks about itself, its defining controversies, and its animating values.

So too with the scholarship of teaching and learning, in which, I will argue, ethical issues are not simply occasions for caution but windows into our values and aspirations as teachers and scholars of teaching.

Trends and Context

That ethical issues should arise in the scholarship of teaching and learning is not to suggest that something is amiss. On the contrary. Attention to ethics is something we *expect* as a field of study or practice evolves and matures. A self-conscious "commitment to integrity" is evoked in the very "ideal of professionalism," William Sullivan observes in *Work and Integrity: The Crisis and Promise of Professionalism in America* (Sullivan, 1995: xvi), and most professions have developed some mechanism—an ethical code or statement of principles—for addressing and dealing with the complicated choices that arise in practice. Thus, one context for understanding the emergence of ethical issues in the scholarship of teaching and learning is as a reflection of the field's development. As more faculty, in more settings and more disciplines, become involved in the work, and as more events, publications, and policies are put in place to support it, attention to ethical issues is a natural development in the scholarship of teaching and learning.

A second context for understanding the emergence of ethical issues is the involvement of doctoral institutions, which are—to the surprise of some observers—well represented in the scholarship of teaching and learning. Slightly more than half of the 114 Carnegie Scholars teach at doctoral institutions, and that sector constitutes almost one-third of the 200 institutions participating in CASTL's Campus Program. Involvement from this set of institutions may well shift the scholarship of teaching and learning—which might be said to exist on a continuum, from informal reflection on one end to more formal research on the other—toward research. With this shift come the benefits of prestige and recognition, but it brings with it as well the traditional machinery of research, including policies and structures (Institutional Review Boards, most notably) for monitoring ethical issues. And while there are issues raised by the investigation of classroom practice that fall outside the usual parameters of IRBs, regulations about "informed consent" for work with "human subjects" raise the visibility of a wider set of ethical issues as well.

Third, the emergence of ethical issues reflects a more general raised awareness and concern about research with human subjects today. The much publicized death of a young woman in a clinical trial at Johns Hopkins University during the summer of 2001 comes to mind. But that case was, in fact, only one of a number of high-profile research-ethics violations, or alleged violations, over the last decade. In the mid-1990s, President Clinton appointed a special commission to study the protection of human subjects in radiation experiments, but the recommendations that resulted were more general, pointing to the need for updated interpretations of federal rules on ethics and more oversight of the system regulating human research (Faden, 1995). By 1998 at least four separate special committees and panels had urged better safeguards at the federal level (Campbell, 1998). A recent report from the American Association of University Professors summarizes the situation by noting that regulations for work with human subjects "have been in place, in one form or another, for more than thirty years. They are a permanent feature of research institutions in the United States, and there are clear signs that their influence is expanding" (AAUP, 2001: 4–5).

Meanwhile, higher education is marked by increased attention to legal issues raised by our work as educators and scholars. In a session at the Carnegie Foundation in summer 2001, a Carnegie Scholar in law reported that her campus (a large doctoral university) now requires written permission to share student work, even anonymously, with other students in the class (for instance as a model answer, or one that raises important issues for the course). "We never had to do that before," the Scholar told us. Similar stories abound. Practices such as posting grades on office doors have become problematic in many settings, for example. A recent (February 2002) U.S. Supreme Court ruling confirms that having students see and evaluate one another's work (for instance in a collaborative learning context) does not violate student privacy, but that once work becomes part of an official record (e.g., a mark in a grade book) it may be protected by the Family Educational Record and Protection Act (Gose, 2002: A25). Moreover, especially as the work of teaching and learning occurs increasingly online, campuses are debating issues about ownership of courses and course materials,

and related matters of intellectual property. In short, there's a whole host of new questions facing higher education, many of them directly related to teaching and learning, and many at the intersection of legal and ethical concerns. Clearly, ethical issues faced by scholars of teaching and learning must be seen in the context of these larger, shifting forces and realities.

Ethical Dilemmas and Competing Goods

But what, in particular, are the issues faced by scholars of teaching and learning? To answer this question—and to do so in a way that recognizes the importance of context in raising and shaping thought about ethical matters—I asked seven Carnegie Scholars, from seven different fields and quite different institutional contexts, to write short case studies about an ethical issue or issues they confronted in their work. Additionally, we invited responses to each case from three individuals who bring different perspectives to bear. This case-plus-commentaries format enacts a central theme of the volume, which is that there's no single right way to resolve the ethical dilemmas that arise when investigating classroom practice; indeed, the most important resource may be awareness and reflection. Though none of the seven case-study authors claims to have found a perfect solution to the ethical dilemmas she or he faced, all have produced work that is highly ethical in its respect for students, its commitment to advancing the profession of teaching, and its thoughtfulness about resolving what are essentially competing goods. Among them, the seven cases embody a number of issues that arise at various points in the scholarship of teaching and learning, from initial design to the sharing of results.

Issues arising at the design stage are a focus in several of the cases. Statistics professor John Holcomb, for instance, naturally thinks of undertaking his investigation—he is interested in the impact of a new approach on students' ability to "actually *do* statistics"—through a classic control-group design; it's a model his field finds credible and familiar. But as he works to refine his plan, and talks to colleagues in other fields, he begins to wonder if that design is the right one. Control group conditions are notoriously difficult to enact in the messy world of the classroom, so there is, for starters, a practical difficulty ("I would be comparing apples and oranges," Holcomb writes). But, even if the practical problem could be overcome, he's not sure a control group is appropriate. "I ran into this wall when I asked myself whether it would be ethical to require students from a traditional course to perform in a way that they had no preparation for." Further, he worries whether it makes sense, ethically, to subject one set of students to an approach he no longer feels confident in, or enthusiastic about. Holcomb's answer is no—and his case thus opens up the relationship between ethical and methodological matters as we see how ethical commitments and values shape the way scholarship of teaching and learning is designed and undertaken.

Issues related to methods of inquiry, and to data collection, are central to several of the cases. Charles McDowell's research design—he is looking at the effectiveness of "pair programming," in which computer science students work together on programming assignments—includes a comparison group (not a formal control group but two settings similar enough to allow analysis of differences), and he is comfortable with that decision. What's less comfortable is the dilemma that emerges as he begins to gather data. Is it appropriate, he wonders, to use class time—even only a few minutes—to gather data for his research when doing so will not advance the learning of students currently enrolled in the class? Is the uncertain prospect of benefits for future students sufficient justification for spending class time in ways that have no immediate pedagogical benefit? Or—as one of McDowell's respondents suggests—is there a way to gather needed data that will actually contribute to student learning? (And might he be mistaken, I would ask, in thinking that his data gathering—a short survey of student work habits—has no pedagogical value?) Additionally, McDowell worries about a dilemma that another Carnegie Scholar, writing in an earlier Carnegie publication, describes as a "changing script." "I was teaching the class *as* I was experimenting with it and studying it," writes Bill Cerbin, a professor of psychology at the University of Wisconsin–La Crosse, "and under those conditions you sometimes *have* to change the script as you go because your best judgment tells you that a change would be an improvement for the students" (Cerbin, 2000: 16). What's at issue in Cerbin's quote, and in McDowell's case, is a conflict between the research role and the role of teacher.

Not surprisingly, the researcher-teacher conflict runs through several of the cases. David Takacs, for instance, team teaches with Gerald Shenk (another Carnegie Scholar) a course on the social and environmental history of California that requires students to explore personal values and commitments. "We subscribe to the feminist aphorism that the personal is political," he points out. "And so we ask—require—that students put themselves into their work." Such a course requires trust between faculty and students, and Takacs worries about "whether students will trust us if they know that we might 'use' their work to further our own scholarship." His solution is to talk with students about his scholarship of teaching and learning throughout the semester—he is interested in how students use history in the "Historically Informed Political Project" they are required to complete—but request permission to use student work only at the end of the semester (and with several options and safeguards built in for students who are uncomfortable with this idea). But, as he points out, "We're still feeling our way through this."

Suzanne Burgoyne faces a similar dilemma in her investigation of a course in Theatre of the Oppressed, where she hopes to study, with a multidisciplinary team of research colleagues, the course's impact on student attitudes toward race and racial oppression. In particular, she worries that the process for securing students' informed consent at the beginning of the study, as prescribed by the Institutional Review Board (it was, she says, "a given that our work would need to go through that process"), will put a chill in the air, making it difficult for students to engage in the emotionally "risky" learning that is required by Theatre of the Oppressed (for instance, in theatre exercises focused on rape, a topic chosen by students but a difficult one for many of them). Relatedly, Burgoyne is aware of issues of power and authority in the classroom, especially when, after an unexpected classroom incident causes the team to

> Holcomb's case opens up the relationship between ethical and methodological matters as we see how ethical commitments and values shape the way scholarship of teaching and learning is designed and undertaken.

refocus its investigation slightly, she finds herself wanting to use data from a student who had previously declined to participate in the study.

Both Burgoyne and Takacs are concerned with power in the classroom. "Teaching should be about challenging, not ossifying, power relations," Takacs says, "and the scholarship of teaching and learning should be the same." An aspect of the scholarship of teaching and learning where issues of power are particularly notable is around the use of student work—an issue that virtually all of the case authors face in one way or another. The form that Takacs and his team-teaching colleague have devised to secure student permission gives three choices: Students can give permission to use their work anonymously, permission to use work with attribution, or no permission. A student volunteer collects the forms and Takacs and Shenk see them only after grades are submitted. But as many of the case authors suggest, this remains tricky territory. How free do students feel to say no? Even if permission is not sought until after grades are turned in, might faculty not have power over the student at a later point—in a subsequent course, for instance? And how "informed" is student consent? How much do or can students really understand about how their work might be used? How does one balance the need to protect students' privacy with the desire to give credit and acknowledgment for the contribution their work makes to the scholarship of teaching and learning? Whose work is it, anyway?

The relationship between teacher and student is also a focus of the case by Tomás Galguera, a faculty member in teacher education, who begins his case by noting, "I have often informed my decisions concerning ethical research issues by considering the nature of the relationship that I have with the people involved in my research." As we soon see, "in researching one's own teaching practice in ways that include students and their work, it is impossible to separate the research from the relationships." Thus, for Galguera, what begins as a teacher-student relationship evolves into a research project—a case study of the development of a Latina elementary school

> How much do or can students really understand about how their work might be used? How does one balance the need to protect students' privacy with the desire to give credit and acknowledgment for the contribution their work makes to the scholarship of teaching and learning? Whose work is it, anyway?

teacher, Camila Calica. As one of the respondents to Galguera's case reports (and Galguera agrees), the negotiation of these various roles is potentially complicated by issues of age, gender, and ethnicity. "I wonder," Galguera says, "whether Camila truly had an opportunity to decline to participate in the study." And he wonders too (once again ethical and methodological issues are hard to separate) whether his close relationship with Camila biases his results—or more deeply informs them.

Galguera raises a different issue as he reflects on sharing the results of his work with a larger audience—an aspect of the scholarship of teaching and learning that raises questions for several of the case writers. On the one hand, he is eager to publish his report, hoping to contribute to current thinking about "the learning-to-teach process for Latina beginner teachers." On the other, he is "curious and

a bit concerned" about what Camila herself will think about the case (a question her commentary in this volume addresses). In particular he wonders if he should have insisted more vigorously about the potential benefits of her playing a more active role as co-presenter and co-author. The work clearly benefits Galguera (one of his initial motivations in undertaking the study was an upcoming tenure decision), but he is less sure what benefit comes to Camila.

The flip side of the "who benefits" issue is a concern about who might be put at risk by the scholarship of teaching and learning, and this is a focus of the case by James Seitz as he recounts dilemmas he faced in writing a book about literacy. Recognizing that investigations of teaching and learning cannot focus exclusively on successes, or feature only the best examples of student work, Seitz rejects the "standard narrative" in which, "at the beginning of the semester, students were struggling ... then the teacher helped them see the light ... and now, as evidence of how far they progressed, the teacher offers a sample of student writing that displays notable accomplishment, thereby demonstrating the success of the teacher's pedagogy." Reading the case, it's easy to imagine that Seitz experiences such successes, but his interest as a scholar of teaching and learning is not so much in success as in the telling difficulties we see in students' learning. The dilemma comes from the fact that he must, therefore, quote from and display "inadequate" student writing, "writing that would be shared not because of its accomplishment but because of its failure." Like several of the other case authors, he wonders about the issue of consent to use student work. Had students known the context in which their work would be shown, would they, he wonders, have given permission? He worries as well about the consequences of his work in the wider public sphere—and about what Thomas Newkirk calls "the ethics of bad news" (Newkirk, 1996: 3). Might his work—though aimed ultimately at improving student literacy—contribute to the "endless river of publications" that bemoan the state of literacy and make a mockery of students? In short, Seitz puts into the picture a whole host of issues about the impact of the scholarship of teaching and learning on the public perception of and support for education.

Issues related to audience perception are also on Sherry Linkon's mind as she recounts her experience of going public with the scholarship of teaching and learning. As part of her work in the Visible Knowledge Project (directed by one of her respondents, Randy Bass, at Georgetown University, and focused on student learning through technology in history and culture courses), Linkon works with a videographer (John Stern, who also responds to her case) to tape a work session by two of her students as they examine and draw inferences from an online nineteenth-century map. When she then shows the video to a group of project colleagues, inviting them to use the work of her students as a way to raise questions about student learning, she is disturbed to find that her sense of the video is not shared by her audience. While she finds it (and means it to be) a way of highlighting "some issues related to prior knowledge and the value of teaching about local culture," her audience laughs at the students. And though this was not their only reaction (good questions were also raised), it is a troubling one. "One of the guiding principles ... of using students' work," Linkon writes, "is that we should treat it and them with respect, and our responses to the video clips were not very respectful." Ultimately her case, like

INTRODUCTION

Seitz's, raises ethical issues about the context in which our investigations of teaching and learning are seen (or read), understood, and used.

There are, certainly, ethical issues that are not raised by the seven cases. And I have not mentioned all of the issues that *are* raised. In practice, of course, they do not appear so discretely as this discussion suggests; each issue spills into others. Standing back from the details of the seven cases, however, one crosscutting theme in particular stands out for me, and it's captured nicely in an essay from Gesa Kirsch and Peter Mortensen's collection *Ethics and Representation in Qualitative Studies of Literacy*: "Presumably, no researcher sets out to be unethical or to hurt those involved in research," writes Helen Dale.

> *Rather, qualitative researchers often must make decisions in which one individual's or group's needs take precedence over those of another individual or group. The choices researchers make are not between good and evil, but between two goods. This creates dilemmas of fidelity. (Dale, 2000: 78)*

What's at issue in the seven cases are not abstract rules of right and wrong but dilemmas of fidelity, attempts to balance competing goods—and to do so in a context without clear norms or rules. As Suzanne Burgoyne notes about her case, "I wouldn't necessarily want to draw a general principle or rule from this narrative." As in most aspects of teaching, what's needed is professional judgment, which is developed at least in part through discussion with scholarly and professional colleagues—which brings us to the topic of the campus context in which scholars of teaching and learning do their work.

Campus Contexts and Communities

Many readers will come to this volume with questions not only about their practice as individual scholars of teaching and learning but about campus processes and policies for addressing ethical issues. An informal survey of 114 Carnegie Scholars in the fall of 2001 (about half returned email questionnaires) revealed that campus approaches vary widely and are under discussion.

Perhaps the most common topic of discussion concerns the role of Institutional Review Boards, though smaller, less research-focused campuses may not have such structures. Institutional Review Boards, as many readers will know, are the mechanism through which the federal government seeks to ensure that the research it funds is carried out in an ethical fashion. That is, campuses conducting federally funded research must establish and maintain an IRB to oversee ethical issues in keeping with the federal regulations. The goal is to protect human subjects against a variety of risks and dangers, from physical and psychological harm to coercion and violations of privacy. Thus, for IRB approval, the investigator must assure that risks to human subjects are minimized, and that those risks that *do* exist are reasonable in relation to the importance of the knowledge that is expected to result; informed consent must be sought from each prospective subject. There are approximately 4000 IRBs in operation today, some in hospitals and research facilities, but most on research university campuses (AAUP, 2001: 2). Some campuses have more than one IRB, in order to specialize in particular areas of research.

Historians of IRB policies note that the first set of principles guiding researchers conducting experiments with human subjects date back to the Nuremberg Code in 1948, which established stan-

dards for judging physicians and scientists who had conducted experiments on concentration camp prisoners. (For an excellent description of the origin and development of IRBs, see Paul Anderson, in Mortensen and Kirsch; also the 2001 AAUP report, "Protecting Human Beings," available online at www.aaup.org/repirb.htm.) Since then, numerous federal regulations have been enacted and updated, the most recent from the Department of Health and Human Services.

As might be expected given the origin of the federal regulations, IRBs are geared especially toward clinical and biomedical research, and disciplines engaged in qualitative research have expressed concern about the appropriateness of those regulations to their work. "Protecting Human Beings," the 2001 report from the American Association of University Professors—sponsored by the American Anthropological Association, the American Historical Association, the American Political Science Association, the American Sociological Association, the Oral History Association, and the Organization of American Historians—explores whether federal regulations, as enacted through Institutional Review Boards, pose obstacles to emergent forms of social science research. "The government imposes a regulatory burden on research institutions and their individual researchers. Whether the burden is reasonable depends on several considerations, not the least of which is the application of the government's rules to disparate academic fields, each with its own concepts and methods of research and standards of professional responsibility" (1). The report reflects "concerns of social scientists that institutional review boards (IRBs) go too far in regulating their research" (AAUP, 2001: 1–2), and a number of recommendations are made for mitigating this situation.

By law, the authority of the IRB extends only to federally funded research. But institutions are also required to develop a mechanism for dealing with non–federally funded research; thus on many campuses, IRB regulations are also employed in other, non–federally funded research. Approximately 75 percent of the largest American research institutions

> What's at issue in the seven cases are not abstract rules of right and wrong but dilemmas of fidelity, attempts to balance competing goods—and to do so in a context without clear norms or rules. As in most aspects of teaching, what's needed is professional judgment...

have voluntarily extended the IRB system to all human-subject research (AAUP, 2001: 3), including, potentially, that which focuses on students and their learning.

Which brings us to the scholarship of teaching and learning. To what extent does IRB oversight pertain to the work of faculty investigating practice in their own settings? A careful reading of the current federal policy for the protection of human subjects suggests that the scholarship of teaching and learning likely is exempt. The projects of the seven Carnegie Scholars featured in this volume, for instance, all would seem to meet the federal policy's exemption requirement for work "conducted in established or commonly accepted educational settings, involving normal educational practices," focused on "effectiveness of or the comparison among instructional techniques, curricula, or classroom management

methods" (see accompanying box for fuller text regarding exempt research). However, "the Federal Policy gives the final judgment to each local IRB" (Anderson, 2000: 276).

Moreover, the meaning of "exempt" is open to misunderstanding. To be exempt, work typically must be *declared* exempt; that is, it is up to the IRB, not to the researcher, to declare the work exempt, which in turn means that appropriate paperwork must be filed (Anderson, 2000: 260; AAUP, 2001: 6). Often the review of projects in the scholarship of teaching and learning will be "expedited," meaning that the IRB chair or spokesperson can sign off on it, and that it does not need to go through the entire committee. But given the volume of work facing such boards, expedited does not necessarily mean speedy. One Carnegie Scholar reports that expedited review of her scholarship of teaching and learning proposal took several months.

Is such review—expedited or not—necessary? Among faculty and campuses I have talked with, there is currently no consensus about this. My survey of Carnegie Scholars suggests that the trend may,

> **Federal Code**
>
> Unless otherwise required by Department or Agency heads, research activities in which the only involvement of human subjects will be in one or more of the following categories are exempt from this policy:
>
> (1) Research conducted in established or commonly accepted educational settings, involving normal educational practices, such as (i) research on regular and special education instructional strategies, or (ii) research on the effectiveness of or the comparison among instructional techniques, curricula, or classroom management methods.
>
> (2) Research involving the use of educational tests (cognitive, diagnostic, aptitude, achievement), survey procedures, interview procedures or observation of public behavior, unless: (i) information obtained is recorded in such a manner that human subjects can be identified, directly or through identifiers linked to the subjects; and (ii) any disclosure of the human subjects' responses outside the research could reasonably place the subjects at risk of criminal or civil liability or be damaging to the subjects' financial standing, employability, or reputation.
>
> (3) Research involving the use of educational tests (cognitive, diagnostic, aptitude, achievement), survey procedures, interview procedures, or observation of public behavior that is not exempt under paragraph (b)(2) of this section, if: (i) the human subjects are elected or appointed public officials or candidates for public office; or (ii) Federal statute(s) require(s) without exception that the confidentiality of the personally identifiable information will be maintained throughout the research and thereafter.
>
> (4) Research involving the collection or study of existing data, documents, records, pathological specimens, or diagnostic specimens, if these sources are publicly available or if the information is recorded by the investigator in such a manner that subjects cannot be identified, directly or through identifiers linked to the subjects. (Code of Federal Regulations, Title 45, Part 46, 2001)

however, be toward IRB involvement, with approximately two-thirds of those from campuses that have such structures indicating that "it is now assumed on my campus that Institutional Review Board approval would be required." As one respondent noted, "It used to be that educational research was exempt on our campus. If you were doing research on your own classroom you didn't have to go through the Institutional Review Board. At about the time I got involved in the scholarship of teaching and learning, that changed." At the same time, however, a number of respondents indicated that they were not sure what was required, or indicated that the matter was under discussion. In fact, a number of approaches are now taking shape on campuses.

The value of collaboration and communication in shaping useful approaches is illustrated by developments at Indiana University, where a high-profile effort to promote and support the scholarship of teaching and learning (and an energetic response from many faculty) raised questions about institutional policy regarding research with human subjects—questions and then distress when it became clear that IRB regulations about research in situations of differential power, such as in studies that focus on one's own students, would make that research more difficult than many faculty members had anticipated. Since then, leaders of the campus's scholarship of teaching and learning initiative have worked in partnership with the IRB to develop a new policy that is cautionary but legitimizing:

> *No matter how well intentioned the teacher is, students may feel compelled to participate, believing that failure to do so will negatively affect their grades.... The Committee recognizes, however, that in some research situations, use of one's own students is integral to the research. This is particularly true of research into teaching methods, curricula and other areas related to the scholarship of teaching and learning. (Indiana University Office of Research and University Graduate School, 2000)*

The institution is actively cultivating a dialogue among IRB members and scholars of teaching and learning so as to develop viable policies and procedures for research in this area. The IRB has clarified some of these issues, including data collection by a third party, data collection by the instructor, and problem practices. Further, the director of the scholarship of teaching and learning initiative serves as a kind of facilitator in discussions between faculty and the IRB, helping faculty frame work in ways that meet IRB requirements and helping IRB members, in turn, understand the work of scholars of teaching and learning. The scholarship of teaching and learning initiative has also developed its own Web page to demystify the human-subjects approval process (Scholarship of Teaching & Learning at Indiana University, 2002).

A very different approach is in force at a liberal arts institution on the west coast, where IRB approval is not only not required, but discouraged. According to a faculty member I talked with, the scholarship of teaching and learning is considered a form of "program assessment" and as such exempt from IRB review. The thinking is that "we don't get student consent to assess our programs and courses, and there's a worry about setting a precedent for getting consent." The campus is discussing the possibility of seeking a kind of blanket permission from all first-year students—but other options are being considered as well.

Yet another approach has taken shape at Mills College. Prompted by new policies requiring review of all student research, education faculty worked with the IRB to define guidelines for the department. These guidelines followed federal regulations and were scrutinized by college lawyers. Additionally, faculty within the teacher preparation program of the education department have created a statement of values that frames the work by faculty and students as informed by and open for inquiry. All members of the program, including students, understand this.

Similarly, the Teacher Education Seminar of the Action Research Collaborative in St. Louis, Missouri, set out to "perhaps, revise the university IRB process to make it more appropriate for action research." Though the idea of an alternative human subject review process did not materialize, the group devised its own set of "Questions for Review and Reflection" to help members focus on ethical issues (Zeni, 2001: 156–164). The questions that appear at the end of this volume reflect a similar effort.

Other approaches are also in evidence. At Portland State University faculty participants in the Scholarship of Teaching Resource Team serve as consultants to one another on a variety of topics, including ethical issues. At Purdue University, the Teaching Academy has taken active leadership in influencing campus policy on ethical issues in the scholarship of teaching and learning. Acknowledging "increased scrutiny throughout the academy on research involving human subjects," participants in the Visible Knowledge Project (the initiative in which Sherry Linkon's case is set) are contributing to a "resource kit" including accounts of the experiences of project members with the IRB process at their own schools.

What's clear from these examples is that campus policies and processes for dealing with ethical issues in the scholarship of teaching and learning are both varied and evolving. As is true in the cases of individual practice, there's no one right approach. What's important—and also most encouraging—is that discussions are now underway, and different approaches are being tried and can be learned from.

Professional Commitments and Aspirations

Ethical issues in the scholarship of teaching and learning do not exist in isolation. They emerge in a larger context of policies and concerns related to research and its changing face. They also reflect the context of teaching practice itself and changing classroom approaches. As one Carnegie Scholar noted in a discussion to brainstorm ideas for this volume, "These issues are a doorway into the heart of what I do as a teacher." Three themes seem particularly important in this context.

The Classroom as a Public Space

One of the fundamental tenets of the scholarship of teaching and learning is "going public"—that is, documenting and representing our work as teachers, and our students' learning, in ways that can be peer reviewed and built upon. As the cases in this volume suggest, and as discussions about human subjects and informed consent on campuses reflect, this idea brings challenges; the privacy of students and their right to learn must be protected. What's also clear is that there's little shared understanding of the status (public vs. private) of what goes on in the classroom: Are the transactions among students and faculty, and the work that students do in the classroom, a form of privileged communication, on an analogy with the work of a therapist or lawyer? Or are they (can they be) "community property" (Shulman, 1993: 6)? What are the boundaries between public and private? Who decides? These are questions for continuing discussion among scholars of teaching and learning.

And yet it's useful to see these questions about the public or private character of the classroom not only in the context of the scholarship of teaching and learning but also through the lens of current thinking about pedagogy itself. Collaborative and cooperative learning, for instance, and many of the active pedagogies now in evidence, entail a shift toward practices that frame the classroom as a space where students are involved in one another's work as a community of learners, engaged in the collaborative construction of knowledge. The work in such classrooms is therefore, in a very real sense, public work. Where that work also engages with outside communities, for instance through service learning, this shift is even more evident. Further, new uses of technology reinforce these directions. In a piece entitled "Teaching

and Learning in the Computer Age: Primacy of Process," Trent Batson and Randy Bass describe how electronic technologies have made the processes of learning and teaching more visible and public. As their students begin to "surf the web," for instance, "the four walls of the classroom may be breaking down more quickly than teachers had thought they would." The result is that faculty in many fields are seeing fundamental changes in "the way knowledge is conceived, challenged, justified and disseminated" (Batson and Bass, 1996: 44). In such a context, issues of privacy, and therefore issues about the use of student work, may take on a different look. One might argue, in fact, that the traditional ways of looking at and dealing with ethical issues in the scholarship of teaching and learning are based on an out-of-date pedagogical model. Perhaps what's needed is a way of framing ethical issues in the scholarship of teaching and learning that is better matched to emerging ideas about the classroom and classroom practice.

Students as Scholars

A related theme pertains to the role of students in the knowledge building that is central to the scholarship of teaching and learning (and to learning itself, for that matter). Many of the faculty I have spoken with find it off-putting to refer to students as "research subjects." As one Carnegie Scholar noted in a planning session for this volume, "For me it's more ethical to treat my students as co-investigators and collaborators, as I would any other scholar." In this sense, the scholarship of teaching and learning may be seen as a cousin to the undergraduate-research movement—in which (at its best) students work collaboratively with faculty, and often with each other as well, to investigate and build knowledge about important issues in the field. Barbara Cambridge, director of CASTL's Campus Program, has been a vigorous proponent of involving students in just this way in the scholarship of teaching and learning (see box), and some campuses have designed programs that do so. At Western Washington University, for instance, faculty decided that questions about teaching and learning were a proper and significant focus not only for faculty scholarship but for student inquiry, creating a special seminar for students interested in studying their learning and the campus context for learning; almost immediately the seminar was over-enrolled. At Elon College the scholarship of teaching and learning means faculty-student study teams working together on course development projects. The point here is that the scholarship of teaching and learning might well be framed not as a particular kind of faculty research, with attendant methods and ethical guidelines, but as a commitment to a different role for students in shaping the education they are a part of.

> **Involving Students**
>
> Done well, undergraduate research is a form of active learning that contributes to deep understanding. In most disciplines, faculty have to this point conducted research with undergraduates that includes the students doing ongoing laboratory work, helping to check sources for a book project, or being part of fieldwork. Few faculty have considered the rich possibilities of undergraduate research in teaching and learning....
>
> This kind of research has the powerful advantage of creating new knowledge for the discipline while enabling student researchers to become more aware of their own process of learning and the circumstances under which they can best learn....
>
> —Cambridge, *AAHE Bulletin*, Volume 52, No. 4, December 1999, page 9–10.

INTRODUCTION

There's an interesting next step in this logic. If students can contribute to the scholarship of teaching and learning (not simply serve as its "subjects"), we should perhaps be concerned not only about protecting their privacy but about acknowledging their *contributions*. "There is a longstanding practice among qualitative researchers to protect the identity and privacy of research participants," writes Cheri Williams.

> *But the practice of preserving informant anonymity often presents perplexing ethical dilemmas for those who conduct ethnographies and case study research. While most researchers disguise participants' names and association to protect them from potential embarrassment or harm, this strategy also prevents participants from receiving recognition. ... [It] eliminates any opportunity for public acknowledgement or praise.* (Williams, 1996: 41)

A number of scholars from composition studies (where the use of student texts in scholarly work is standard procedure) are avid about this, arguing that we have an ethical responsibility to acknowledge and cite student work as we would that of any scholar who contributed to our thinking. (For examples, see Gesa Kirsch's description of "multivocal texts" in *Ethical Dilemmas in Feminist Research*.) This approach will appeal more in some fields than others, and it is not without its problems, but it offers a different lens for thinking about ethical issues. Students might well help shape our inquiries, contribute to the collection and analysis of data, and play important roles in interpreting and sharing results with various audiences. In this sense the scholarship of teaching and learning may be an important way to make students more "intentional learners," "meaning they are purposeful and reflective, both about the use of their learning and the process of gaining it," as urged in a new report from the Association of American Colleges and Universities (Association of American Colleges and Universities, 2002: 2).

An Ethic of Inquiry

This volume focuses on ethical issues in the scholarship of teaching and learning—the "ethics of inquiry," as the title says. But a slight shift of language captures one of the larger themes that emerges here. An *ethic* of inquiry, that is, puts the emphasis not so much on specific issues to be grappled with but on a larger sense of professional responsibility and aspiration that motivates and shapes the scholarship of teaching and learning. Existing codes of ethics for teachers emphasize diligence in preparing for class, timely return of student work, respect for students, and other important elements of professional practice. But the scholarship of teaching and learning enacts an additional kind of professional responsibility by calling on the inherent obligations and commitments that come with the professorial role—that is, to seek knowledge, to share what our investigations uncover, and to contribute to the larger community of scholars and practitioners. In the case of the scholarship of teaching and learning this means approaching our students' learning with the same spirit of disciplined inquiry with which we approach other aspects of our scholarly work. That ethic is what animates the work of the case authors represented in this volume, and it is what Lee Shulman describes as "the professional rationale" for the scholarship of teaching and learning, work that *affords all of us the opportunity to enact the functions of scholarship for which we were all prepared. We can treat our courses and classrooms as laboratories or field sites in the best sense of the term, and can contribute through our scholarship to the improvement and understanding of learning and teaching in our field. (Shulman, 2000: 50)*

The scholarship of teaching and learning is, in this sense, a moral commitment, a responsibility "to our professional peers to 'pass on' what we discover, discern, and experience" in working with our students (Shulman, 2000: 50). Rather than a new research specialty for a few faculty, it is, I would argue, an aspiration for the work of all faculty—one that enacts responsibilities both to current students and to future generations; to colleagues, whose work we build on and contribute to; and to the profession of teaching.

The Aims of This Volume

This introduction attempts to provide a broad overview of the "ethics of inquiry," identifying issues that arise for faculty investigating their own classrooms, placing those issues in the context of campus policies and federal regulations, and highlighting themes that provide different perspectives on the topic. I want to end on a more concrete, practical note by making a few comments about the aims of this volume and what you'll find in the pages that follow.

Most of the volume consists of the seven cases and commentaries described earlier in this introduction. Their purpose is to name and illustrate some of the issues faced by scholars of teaching and learning, and to create a forum for discussing those issues from diverse points of view.

Readers are invited to use the cases to start discussions in their own settings—among faculty colleagues, administrators and staff, IRB members, and students. Items listed in the Annotated Bibliography at the end of the volume (and in the resources that accompany each case) can help inform those discussions, as well.

The cases may also serve as models for further case writing. As all of the authors and respondents would, I believe, agree, case writing prompts analysis and reflection that's helpful both for the author and for readers who engage with the cases. Inviting faculty to develop and share cases about ethical dilemmas they face in their scholarship of teaching and learning may be a good first step toward formulating appropriate practices and policies on your campus.

Though the cases are not meant to provide "answers," they *are* meant to be a source of practical suggestions and guidance. For example, David Takacs shares a form he uses to seek students' permission to use their work. (Further examples of forms are available on the CD-ROM that accompanies a previous Carnegie publication, *Opening Lines: Approaches to the Scholarship of Teaching and Learning*.) Helen Neville, in her response to Suzanne Burgoyne, suggests working with a collaborative team of researchers, who can, together, troubleshoot and resolve ethical dilemmas that may be more difficult if you're working alone. Respondents to Sherry Linkon's case offer wise advice about the need to frame and contextualize evidence about student learning—especially evidence such as video that lends itself to multiple interpretations. Peter Alexander's response to Charles McDowell's case suggests ways to make data-gathering an educationally valuable experience for students. Indeed, many of the authors

point to the value of involving students in the scholarship of teaching and learning; students can help frame questions, gather data, and apply findings.

Also helpful in a practical way, I hope, will be the Questions to Shape Practice that appear following the cases. They can be used by individuals to raise awareness of ethical issues but might also provide a framework for discussion with colleagues engaged in the scholarship of teaching and learning. Please feel free to copy (or adapt) and use the questions in campus conversations and other contexts.

Finally it's important to say that this volume is meant as a resource, not a final statement. As noted at the beginning of this essay, attention to the "ethics of inquiry" is a natural development in the evolution of the scholarship of teaching and learning. The issues are complicated but they needn't be paralyzing. Even more, they are interesting issues, and important ones that deserve attention and discussion. The problems we pose as scholars of teaching and learning, the way we frame and investigate them, and the ways in which results are shared with others and used are reflections of our values. Rather than seeing ethical issues as problems to be managed, we can, I believe, see them as contexts for expressing what we most care about as educators and professionals.

Resources

Anderson, Paul. "Ethics, Institutional Review Boards, and the Involvement of Human Participants in Composition Research." In P. Mortensen and G. E. Kirsch (eds.), *Ethics and Representation in Qualitative Studies of Literacy*. Urbana, Ill.: National Council of Teachers of English, 1996.

Association of American Colleges and Universities. "Report of the Greater Expectations National Panel, Executive Summary." Draft, distributed at AAHE National Conference on Higher Education, Chicago, Ill., Mar. 2002.

Bass, Randy. "The Scholarship of Teaching: What's the Problem?" *Inventio* 1(1) [http://www.doiiit.gmu.edu/Archives/feb98/randybass.htm]. 1999.

Batson, Trent, and Bass, Randy. "Teaching and Learning in the Computer Age: Primacy of Process." *Change,* 1996, 28(2), 42–47.

Cambridge, Barbara. "The Scholarship of Teaching and Learning: Questions and Answers from the Field." *AAHE Bulletin*, 1999, 52 (4), 7–10.

Campbell, P. W. "Ethics Panel Urges Better Safeguards for Human Research Subjects." *Chronicle of Higher Education*, Daily News, Dec. 10, 1998. [http://chronicle.com/daily/2002].

Cassell, J., and Jacobs, S. E. "Introduction." In J. Cassell and S. E. Jacobs (eds.), *Handbook on Ethical Issues in Anthropology*. Washington, D.C.: American Anthropological Association, 1987. [www.aaanet.org].

Cerbin, William. "Investigating Student Learning in a Problem-Based Psychology Course." In P. Hutchings (ed.), *Opening Lines: Approaches to the Scholarship of Teaching and Learning.* Menlo Park, Calif.: Carnegie Foundation for the Advancement of Teaching, 2000.

Code of Federal Regulations, Title 45, Part 46. "Protection of Human Subjects." Department of Health and Human Services, National Institutes of Health, Office for Protection from Research Risks. Revised November 13, 2001. Effective December 13, 2001. [http://ohrp.osophs.dhhs.gov/humansubjects/guidance/45cfr46.htm].

Dale, Helen. "Dilemmas of Fidelity: Qualitative Research in the Classroom." In P. Mortensen and G. E. Kirsch (eds.), *Ethics and Representation in Qualitative Studies of Literacy.* Urbana, Ill.: National Council of Teachers of English, 1996.

Faden, R. "Protecting Human Subjects." *Chronicle of Higher Education*, Oct. 20, 1995, p. A56.

Gose, B. "Privacy Law Does Not Preclude Use of Student Graders, Supreme Court Rules." *Chronicle of Higher Education*, March 1, 2002, p. A25.

Huber, Mary Taylor, and Morreale, Sherry P. (eds.). *Disciplinary Styles in the Scholarship of Teaching and Learning: Exploring Common Ground.* Washington, D.C.: American Association for Higher Education, 2002.

Mortensen, P., and Kirsch, G. E. (eds). *Ethics and Representation in Qualitative Studies of Literacy.* Urbana, Ill: National Council of Teachers of English, 1996.

Newkirk, Thomas. "Seduction and Betrayal in Qualitative Research." In P. Mortensen and G. E. Kirsch (eds.), *Ethics and Representation in Qualitative Studies of Literacy.* Urbana, Ill.: National Council of Teachers of English, 1996.

Shulman, Lee S. "Teaching as Community Property: Putting an End to Pedagogical Solitude." *Change,* 1993, 25(6), 6–7.

———. "From Minsk to Pinsk: Why a Scholarship of Teaching and Learning?" *Journal of Scholarship of Teaching and Learning (JoSoTL),* 2000, 1(1), 48–51. [http://www.carnegiefoundation.org/CASTL/highered/index.htm].

Sullivan, William. *Work and Integrity: The Crisis and Promise of Professionalism in America.* New York: HarperBusiness, 1995.

Williams, Cheri L. "Dealing with the Data: Ethical Issues in Case Study Research." In P. Mortensen and G. E. Kirsch (eds.), *Ethics and Representation in Qualitative Studies of Literacy.* Urbana, Ill.: National Council of Teachers of English, 1996.

Zeni, J. (ed). *Ethical Issues in Practitioner Research.* New York: Teachers College Press, 2001.

Internet Resources

AAUP (American Association of University Professors). *Protecting Human Beings: Institutional Review Boards and Social Science Research.* Washington, D.C.: American Association of University Professors. [http://www.aaup.org/statements/Redbook/repirb.htm]. 2001.

Center for Academic Excellence: Portland State University. "Center for Academic Excellence (Home)." [www.oaa.pdx.edu/CAE]. N.d.

Indiana University Office of Research and University Graduate School. "Bloomington Campus Committee for the Protection of Human Subjects." [www.indiana.edu/~resrisk/stusub.html]. Nov. 29, 2000.

Scholarship of Teaching & Learning at Indiana University. "Resources Regarding the Protection of Human Subjects in SOTL Research." [www.indiana.edu/~sotl/humansub.html]. Feb. 8, 2002.

Visible Knowledge Project: Learning, Technology, Inquiry. [http://crossroads.georgetown.edu/vkp]. N.d.

CASE one

The Ethics of Comparison:
A Statistician Wrestles with the Orthodoxy of a Control Group

John P. Holcomb Jr.
Mathematics
Cleveland State University

I have been engaged in the scholarship of teaching and learning to assess a new approach in an introductory, elementary statistics course during the 2000-2001 academic year. This is a general service course for non–math or non–statistics majors that's taught all across the country. The approach that I've been using—which is quite different from the way the course is traditionally taught—employs a birth-weight data set that students work with all semester. Using these data, and working in collaborative teams, students do a sequence of four data-analysis projects. Each team then writes a report on its findings. I grade the report with a weight of 50 percent on the writing and presentation and 50 percent on the accuracy of the statistical analysis. What I wanted to do in my scholarship of teaching and learning study was to assess how effective these projects were in helping students learn to actually *do* statistics. And when I say I wanted students to be able to *do* statistics, I mean that I wanted them to be able to analyze data and then communicate their results effectively. So that was my original plan and hope. The challenge was to figure out how to assess the impact of these sequenced, collaborative, written data-analysis projects.

In thinking about how I could accomplish this—how I could assess the impact of this new approach—I found myself thinking about the kind of classically designed experiment that the statistician in me finds very comfortable and familiar, where you give some designated "treatment" to a certain group of people and then

---

John Holcomb, assistant professor of mathematics, is devoted to improving statistics education at the local and national level. He studies and writes about the use of data-oriented learning projects, and has conducted several workshops across the country for teachers wishing to use real data in their classes. He is a 2000 Carnegie Scholar.

Respondents

Roberto L. Corrada is associate professor at the University of Denver College of Law, where he has been teaching civil rights, labor, employment, contract, and administrative law for twelve years. He has written about active and collaborative learning in the law school classroom. He was a Carnegie Scholar in 2000.

Joan Garfield has focused her professional work over the past twenty years on improving the undergraduate teaching of statistics courses. She has collected and conducted research related to teaching and learning statistics, and has written articles and book chapters on statistical reasoning, student assessment, and technology in statistics education. She is currently heading a new graduate program in statistics education at the University of Minnesota.

Caroline Hodges Persell, professor of sociology at New York University, teaches, conducts research, and publishes in the sociology of education, inequality, and the scholarship of teaching and learning. She has won a National Science Foundation Faculty Development Award, was named a Carnegie Scholar in 2000, and is past president of the Eastern Sociological Society.

compare the results with a "control group" that receives a placebo treatment or no treatment at all. But this approach, the more I thought about it, presented both methodological and ethical questions, which are hard to separate from each other.

One thing I realized was that a control group model was not going to be very tenable in my situation because the bottom line—the thing I wanted to analyze—was students' ability to do a data-analysis project, and I couldn't see how to compare the performance of the "treatment group" with performance in a traditionally taught statistics course where students are never taught or asked to do this kind of data analysis. This is partly a methodological problem; I would be comparing apples and oranges. But it also has an ethical dimension. I ran into this wall when I asked myself whether it would be ethical to require students from a traditional course to perform in a way that they had no preparation for. I was concerned that the tasks I would need to have them do would seem completely out of the blue. And, especially because I would have to have students do these tasks in a way that would ensure their full effort (or I wouldn't have good data), the work would have to count toward their final grade in the course. That just didn't seem fair. Asking students to do something they haven't been prepared to do invites poor performance, and it also puts students in a position of feeling incompetent and anxious. My philosophy about this is that you can pose tasks that stretch student thinking but they can't be too far afield from class examples and homework. So, as I say, this is an area where methodological concerns and ethical ones seemed to converge.

There's another dimension to my concern about the use of control groups, as well. It's a concern about bias. That is, if I were teaching both sections of the course—one with the new approach and one on the more traditional model—I would be concerned that my belief in the new method would bias my interpretation of the relative success of the two sections—or, rather, that my bias would be one of the factors determining the relative success. I would be concerned about giving the students in the treatment group more of my attention and energy, and about conveying, even unintentionally, a greater degree of confidence that would somehow put them in a privileged position. One solution to this would be to ask a colleague, or two colleagues, to teach the two versions of the course, so my own biases wouldn't enter in. But in my case this wasn't particularly feasible. I was new to Cleveland State, and I didn't feel I could call on my colleagues, whom I barely knew, in quite this way. I certainly didn't want to ask a colleague to teach in a new way that he or she might not believe in or be comfortable with; we faculty can sabotage a new approach very easily if we aren't persuaded it has potential. And if the new approach didn't work for a colleague, I didn't want to be responsible for that failure. In any event, working with colleagues did not seem like a good option for me, so I was faced with this issue of bias and treating some students—despite my intention to be neutral—in a favored, privileged way.

Of course the flip side of the bias issue is that the control group would be deprived of an experience that I feel is better and more educationally powerful—though at the time I didn't have empirical evidence for this. I've taught with these projects for a couple of years now and I've become increasingly persuaded that they really work. I just couldn't see using a model for my scholarship of teaching that would mean jettisoning this approach. If I really think that the use of these collaborative projects is the best way to teach

statistics, wouldn't it be unethical of me to withhold that approach from some students? A statistics course is not a life-or-death medical situation or a medical clinical study, but I believe this course really does make a difference for students. And they only take it once. If they move on to subsequent courses and my colleagues tell me that the students don't seem well prepared, I would feel ethically responsible for putting them at a disadvantage.

So what did I do in light of these concerns? It wasn't easy for me to let go of the control group model, but I eventually decided not to worry about comparisons. I didn't think it was appropriate to test students in a control group section on something they weren't prepared to do. And I didn't think I could, in good conscience, not teach them in a way that I feel is very powerful. So I simply looked at my own students in the class I was teaching with the collaborative data-analysis projects. Students worked together on the birth-weight data sets in a sequence of problems throughout the semester; these problems were homework. To assess the impact of this ongoing work, I gave each student his or her own data set for the midterm and final and asked for the same kind of analysis, but done independently. That is, the exams covered material very similar to what the students completed for homework assignments in their teams. My outcome measure, then, was the percentage of students completing the midterm and final exams in a satisfactory matter—a sort of "threshold of understanding," which I set at 80 percent. If students could get an 80 or above, then I considered the method successful.

> A statistics course is not a life-or-death medical situation, but I believe this course really does make a difference for students. If they move on to subsequent courses and my colleagues tell me that the students don't seem well prepared, I would feel ethically responsible for putting them at a disadvantage.

By providing an authentic assessment experience with the take-home examinations, I was also able to wed a meaningful evaluation of the effectiveness of the previous homework assignments with an educational experience useful for students. These finished take-home midterms and final examinations provide a written record of student achievement. The results of the take-home final examination showed that 86 percent of the students scored 80 or better, with 49 percent scoring 90 or better. Other teachers can examine these results, together with the final products from the students, and make their own judgment as to the effectiveness of the homework assignments. For me personally, the evaluation convinced me the homework projects are aiding student learning for the vast majority of students. In addition, because the assignments and exams are authentic activities themselves, this study has shown something quite meaningful without a direct comparison to a treatment group. Have I proven anything definitively? No. However, even without a control group, I find the evidence very compelling that the projects are benefiting student learning.

CASE one

Commentary on John Holcomb's Case

Roberto L. Corrada
Law
University of Denver College of Law

John Holcomb's provocative case raises a number of issues regarding the ethics of the scholarship of teaching and learning. I will explore the issue of a control group, which I have thought about and dealt with in the context of my own classroom research. But I want to start by discussing John's concern about asking students to perform in ways that come "out of the blue." My view of this issue is foundational to my perspective on the use of control groups.

In thinking about comparing work by students in his performance-oriented class with work done in a traditional statistics course, John worries about the fairness of requiring students from the traditional class to perform tasks they haven't prepared for. This makes me wonder about the substantive differences in the two classes. Is it that different material is covered in the two classes? Or is it that expectations are different, and, therefore, that different teaching approaches are used?

My guess is that the difference is related primarily to expectations and to their impact on how the class is taught. In his performance-oriented class, John seems to expect more student initiative. In the traditional class, the professor might design a traditional test that leads students from question to question, asking for application of various statistical formulae. The performance-oriented class, on the other hand, involves an actual data set and a series of problems related to that one set. Probably the data set is larger and in a more raw form than found on the traditional exam. Students find it necessary to ask questions (of the professor or each other) about how to manipulate the data and represent the findings. The students are not led as much by the problems (or questions) themselves but must bring more independent thought into what they do.

I have laid the same groundwork and generated the same higher-level expectations in my performance-oriented labor law class. In that class, I invite students to form a union and bargain with me about the terms and conditions of the class. As contrasted with the traditionally taught labor law class, students are required to perform in ways that are less defined. They engage in union organizing, they file for a union election, and then (if the union is voted in) they engage in collective bargaining with me. The students decide, on their own, the thrust of the union campaign and then decide, again on their own, what to ask for in collective bargaining. In the traditional class, the students study cases and extract law from them in order to resolve various hypothetical questions posed to them in a final examination. The final exam tests not only their knowledge of law but also their application of the law to various situations the students have not seen before the exam. The major difference between the two classes is that in the traditional class *I* create the problems, presumably with some solutions or answers based on assigned material. In the performance-oriented class, the class itself *is* the problem. As a result, I teach in a different way. I let the students know the expectations are different. I "scaffold" their learning in different ways (e.g., by providing a link to the National Labor Relations Board Web site). I ask different questions. In light of these differences in teaching approach, it would be unfair to spring a union election on a traditionally taught class *even though I cover the same material*. Ultimately I don't think John or I could make the different assignment fairer to the traditional class without changing the way the class is taught.

At the same time, John's concern about "out of the blue" requirements struck me as curious, because in a sense our goal is to enable students to perform something out of the blue. As a law professor, I want students to be critical thinkers, meaning that they can take what they've learned in class and think through how to apply it correctly in a new or different context. And so, not only is it fair to ask students something "out of the blue," I believe it should be

required. But John's statement hits upon a tension here, one that is both ethical and practical. How much do we tell students (make things visible), and how much do we strive to keep things hidden so that they can discover them on their own? I think true learning comes from discovery, but, as teachers, I believe we are ethically obliged to give students

> As a law professor, I want students to be critical thinkers, meaning that they can take what they've learned in class and think through how to apply it correctly in a new or different context. Not only is it fair to ask students something "out of the blue," I believe it should be required.

the tools they need to learn effectively in this way. As John's case suggests, the proper balance is not an easy one to strike.

This brings me to the issue of the control group. Several years ago, I began to teach labor law in a performance-oriented way using a simulation, which is quite a departure from the traditional lecture and inquiry style that dominates most law classes. Through various qualitative techniques and anecdotal evidence (including student surveys and evaluations, examination responses, and casual discussions), I have become convinced that using a simulation in the labor law class leads to better student learning.

But though I *believe* better learning occurs, I am not yet fully convinced. Thus, I've been attempting more meaningful assessment. Like John, I have been inclined toward a comparative model, and I have faced the same question he faced: How does one create a group for comparison? Though there is no way to "control" for all the important factors and influences, even a rough comparison may raise interesting questions or allow certain suggestive conclusions. Like John, I considered teaching my course in two ways in order to have such a comparison.

However, *I just could not do it*. Though I had resolved to teach one class the traditional way, I found myself switching back to the simulation format at the last minute. Why? Was it because I preferred the simulation approach? No—because although it has the benefit of making the class unpredictable and fresh, the simulation approach is a *lot more work*. I almost always regret the choice to teach the simulation class because of the extra effort involved. Did I feel that my new approach was so much better that I would be shortchanging students if I taught in the traditional way? This cannot explain my choice, either, because I teach Contracts, Administrative Law, and Race Theory in a more traditional style. And scads of labor law professors across the country teach labor law in a lecture-inquiry format; that's the way I learned labor law myself (with apparent success).

When it comes down to it, the reason I could not teach the course in the traditional way is because it didn't *feel* right. Not to use an approach I felt was more promising (though I don't have definitive data yet) would have meant not being true to myself. And my own individual teacher ethic is what keeps me going, working, learning. I fear what would happen if I did not pay attention to it. And so, like John, I have resolved to follow the path dictated by my teacher ethic, even at the cost of a more scientifically accepted research design.

2 Joan B. Garfield
Educational Psychology
University of Minnesota

As I read John Holcomb's case, I immediately recalled an experience I had several years ago when trying to develop a proposal for my doctoral research. I wanted to compare a new problem-solving version of an introductory statistics course to a traditional version of the course. Based on the literature and research in mathematics education advocating problem-solving methods of teaching, I believed that the new version would lead to greater student achievement.

My adviser tried to steer me to a more clearly defined problem to investigate. He suggested that since I already believed that the problem-solving

course would be superior to a traditional course, why not look at different versions of problem-solving courses, and compare them, to see what factors really made a difference in student outcomes. Following his advice, I was able to randomly assign my students to different versions of the treatment, and later compare their achievement using tests that measured different levels of learning. The results were informative and led to continued exploration of instructional methods that can improve student learning, a focus of my scholarship for the past twenty years.

My experience parallels Holcomb's in a number of ways. His first idea of using a "traditional course" as a control group reminded me of my adviser's advice. Comparing a new type of course—often referred to as a "reformed" course—to a "traditional" course presents difficulties. As Holcomb makes clear, there are problems regarding bias, his own belief that his "reformed" course was better than a traditional course, and ethical issues related to our responsibility to give all students the best possible learning experience. Additionally, I would point out that there is not just one type of traditional course. Thus, even if a comparison of a traditional course to a reformed course suggests that the reformed course resulted in higher student achievement, it is difficult to generalize to other types of courses because each "traditional" course is so different. The results of a comparison would only pertain to the exact version of courses used in this comparison, which is not a very useful finding. If Holcomb had compared his new course to a traditional course, he would not have learned what aspect of the courses made a difference in student learning, just that the two courses led to different results.

I was impressed by the solution that Holcomb devised: to teach students in the way he believed to be the most effective and authentic (clearly an ethical decision), and then to assess student outcomes. This requires a clear articulation of learning goals for students. Looking at the impact of a particular instructional method or activity on student outcomes is an example of what is often referred to as classroom research. In classroom research (or action research) studies, an instructor perceives a problem in student learning (e.g., students are not able to analyze data after completing a statistics course), develops an activity or intervention (e.g., Holcomb's sequence of projects), adds this to the course, and then assesses the results. Classroom research is usually a dynamic, ongoing process, and I predict that this is how Holcomb will use the data gathered from his students as well. That is, rather than assess the students once, and make a judgment about the effectiveness of using student projects, Holcomb may realize that there is something else he might do to change the project or a related aspect of instruction. He might then make further additions or revisions and try yet another version of the course with a new class of students. Again, he would assess students, examine the results, and proceed to make further changes. This type of dynamic classroom research is focused on the students and is used to constantly improve instruction and therefore student learning. It is, if you will, an ethical way to teach, in which the teacher takes responsibility for the ongoing improvement of his or her students' learning.

Moreover, this research model may be used collaboratively with other colleagues who teach similar courses, and results can be shared across classrooms. The results of research or evaluation using classroom research methods are immediate, practical, and ethically responsible. Rather than determine if one teaching method is better than another, it focuses on whether or not students are achieving the desired learning outcomes.

This method of research and evaluation is quite different from the formal research-design model learned by statistics students. As a trained statistician, John Holcomb originally wanted to design an experiment with a control group because that is the procedure he was trained to use. Although using this method to compare two different classes did not make sense to him for the reasons he described, there *are* times when certain features of experimental design (random assignment and control groups) can be used to help evaluate the impact of different instructional methods. Sometimes, for instance, there may be small activities or projects that can be undertaken in two variations and compared—for example, having students analyze a set of existing data or having them collect and analyze their own data. The relative power of these two approaches (both of which have their advocates) could be investigated in a small, focused research study. Students could be

randomly assigned to one of the two approaches; then, after the activity, a carefully designed assessment would be given to students to evaluate the effectiveness of the activity. To avoid the ethical issue Holcomb faced (one set of students having a more beneficial experience), each group could later experience the activity used by the other group by being given a second course project. In this way, instructors' beliefs about whether it is more effective to have students analyze data provided by their teacher or to collect and analyze their own data could actually be tested.

Trying out new activities with students raises interesting and important ethical issues. As Holcomb's case and my own comments suggest, ethical issues are also, often, methodological issues. It's difficult to separate the two. A promising approach to both is to follow Holcomb's example, using classroom research and small, focused experiments to study the impact of teaching in ways that can directly improve student learning.

3 Caroline Hodges Persell
Sociology
New York University

John Holcomb's very thoughtful case raises ethical issues about the process of studying students' learning while we are teaching them. He raises both ethical and practical issues surrounding the existence of a control group, and I believe the issues are interrelated. A recurrent theme in the case is John's concern that conducting his research on student learning might somehow harm that learning. He fears students could be hurt if, in order to devise a control group, he were to withhold a form of teaching he believes is efficacious for their learning. Students in turn might be concerned that a new teaching method might hurt their grades, an issue raised by a colleague of mine who was trying an experimental teaching method. My colleague handled this concern by obtaining the grade distributions for prior sections of the similar courses and matching them to the grade distribution in the course he was teaching, so his students' grades, at least, were not affected by the new method.

Medical research is another context in which the ethical problems of control groups arise. I know of medical centers where patients must agree to participate in a medical experiment to obtain treatment. If they agree, patients are randomly assigned to a control group that receives the "best" current medical treatment for their conditions or to an experi-

> John raises both ethical and practical issues surrounding the existence of a control group, and I believe the issues are interrelated. He fears that students could be hurt if he were to withhold a form of teaching he believes is efficacious for their learning.

mental group that receives the latest experimental treatment (which may be better or worse than the current one). Patients are presumably informed of all of this before they proceed, told of possible risks, and given the chance to go elsewhere for the current best treatment. Clearly they might be more willing to participate in such experiments when existing treatments are less than perfect—a situation I think we can safely say describes a good deal of statistics instruction in the United States today, as well. Still, we might ask how such a model could work in education, and whether it would be desirable. The situation John describes did not offer such options, and the approach he was exploring was not totally unknown in the way an experimental drug would be. He and perhaps others in statistics had used the method before. So John knew that at least it would not actively harm students. In fact he believed it was better.

However, I sense that John's struggle with the control group issue speaks not only to its ethical dimensions but to its intellectual and evidentiary importance. As he notes, statisticians feel they are on firmer ground if they have solid evidence for the superiority of one teaching method compared to another. Is it possible to obtain some comparative data by using other cohorts? For example, are there any data on how students who took statistics in the past did in their subsequent courses compared to students taught with this new approach? (Of course there are multiple factors at work, including different instructors, that might explain any differences observed.) An example of how a comparison group might be obtained from prior cohorts is Robert E. Fullilove and Philip Uri Treisman's 1990 article about a special workshop designed to help students struggling with calculus at the University of California, Berkeley. Another possibility might be a quick survey of professors who teach subsequent courses to see if they perceive any differences over time in student capacity to do statistics. Though such measures are likely to underestimate the possible effects of this new teaching approach, positive results would be quite encouraging and would provide somewhat stronger evidence for inferring efficaciousness.

In addition to the ethical and inferential desirability of comparative data, I see this case as suggesting other ethical issues relating to goals and assessment. The goal of this statistics course is having students become able to conduct and interpret statistical analyses—to "actually *do* statistics," as John writes. As he reports, this is different from the goals of a more traditional course. Decisions about the goals of a course are based on values and thus warrant discussion in ethical terms. The choice of competency-based rather than norm-referenced evaluations may also be seen as an ethical decision, although I seldom see it discussed in such terms. Goals and their measurement involve both research and teaching decisions. The issues of what goals and assessments are chosen, how, why, and by whom are extremely worthy of further discussion.

Resources

Cobb, G. "Teaching Statistics." In L. Steen (ed.), *Heeding the Call for Change: Suggestions for Curricular Action*. Mathematical Association of America Notes Series, no. 22. Washington, D.C.: Mathematical Association of America, 1992.

Colvin, S. and Vos, K. E. "Authentic Assessment Models for Statistics Education." In I. Gal and J. Garfield (eds.), *The Assessment Challenge in Statistics Education*. Washington, D.C.: IOS Press, 1997.

Cross, K. Patricia, and Steadman, Mimi Harris. *Classroom Research: Implementing the Scholarship of Teaching*. San Francisco: Jossey-Bass, 1996.

delMas, R. C.; Garfield, J.; and Chance, B. L. "A Model of Classroom Research in Action: Developing Simulation Activities to Improve Students' Statistical Reasoning." *Journal of Statistics Education*, 1999, 7(3). [http://www.amstat.org/publications/jse/secure/v7n3/delmas.cfm].

Fullilove, Robert E., and Treisman, Philip Uri. "Mathematics Achievement Among African American Undergraduates at the University of California, Berkeley: An Evaluation of the Mathematics Workshop Program." *Journal of Negro Education*, 1990, 59(3), 463–478.

Holcomb, John. *Assessing Student Learning in Introductory Statistics*. Course Web page, focused on Holcomb's scholarship of teaching and learning project for Carnegie. [http://academic.csuohio.edu/holcombj/assess]. Spring 2001.

Holcomb J., and Ruffer, R. "Using a Term-Long Project Sequence in Introductory Statistics." *The American Statistician*, 2000, 54, 49–53.

Moore, T. (ed.). *Teaching Statistics: Resources for Undergraduate Instructors*. Mathematical Association of America Notes Series, no. 52. Washington, D.C.: Mathematical Association of America, 2000.

Wiggins, Grant, and McTighe, Jay. *Understanding by Design*. Alexandria, Va.: Association for Supervision and Curriculum Development, 1998.

Wiske, Martha S. *Teaching for Understanding: Linking Research to Practice*. San Francisco: Jossey-Bass, 1998.

CASE two

Using Student Work as Evidence

David Takacs
Environmental Humanities
California State University, Monterey Bay

I am interested in scholarship of teaching and learning projects that aim to improve learning not just of future generations but of present ones, the students with whom I now share a classroom. I worry deeply about the power relations embedded in such scholarship. Teaching should be about challenging, not ossifying, power relations; and the scholarship of teaching and learning should be the same.

How do we "use" student work as evidence in our scholarship of teaching and learning? My colleague Gerald Shenk and I faced a set of ethical questions as we designed our scholarship of teaching and learning and thought about how we might cite student work as evidence.

The context for this work was the course Social & Environmental History of California that Gerald and I team teach; the goal of the course is to help students become ethical, effective, historically informed, and self-aware members of the civic lives of their communities. We wished to use students' final Historically Informed Political Projects (HIPPs) as evidence that they had made progress toward this goal. Do students show a more sophisticated understanding of politics as a result of doing the work for our course? Do they have a firmer grasp of policy issues? Do they express empowerment about making a difference in their communities? Do they show a commitment to continue their work? Do they develop a sophisticated understanding of the connection between values and politics? These were questions we hoped to investigate through examination of the students' work.

David Takacs teaches environmental humanities in the Institute for Earth Systems Science & Policy at California State University, Monterey Bay. As Carnegie Scholars, he and his colleague Gerald Shenk are studying praxis pedagogies to help students become effective, ethical, self-aware members of the civic lives of their communities.

Respondents

Amy Driscoll is director of Teaching, Learning, and Assessment at California State University, Monterey Bay. She presents widely and writes about pedagogy and assessment. Her text *Universal Teaching Strategies* is in preparation for a fourth edition.

Kevin Miller is currently pursuing a bachelor's degree in social and behavioral sciences with a focus on social history at California State University, Monterey Bay. He is a teacher's assistant for a history course entitled Domination and Resistance in the Americas.

Cynthia Scheinberg, associate professor of English at Mills College, has received a number of teaching awards for her work in composition and composition pedagogy, service learning, and Victorian literature. As a 2000 Carnegie Scholar, she is currently at work on a scholarship of teaching and learning project concerning the dynamics of classroom discussions and their relationship to student writing.

But to use their work, we needed their permission. What is the best time to obtain that permission? We want our students to know that we're engaged in this kind of scholarship, but we don't want to do anything that might hamper them from freely expressing themselves in the course. Central to our pedagogy, we subscribe to the feminist aphorism that the personal is political. And so we ask—require—that students put themselves into their work. What are they passionate about, and why? How does this passion inform the political project we ask them to design and conduct? What do they learn about themselves as a result of conducting that project?

In order to express themselves freely, students have to trust us. And we worry about whether they will trust us if they know that we might "use" their work to further our own scholarship. We work hard to build a community of trust in our classrooms, and we remain concerned that the prospect of public display might put a chill on that community, preventing our students from investing themselves fully in their work.

Here is the current solution we've negotiated—and we're still feeling our way through this. We tell students about our scholarship of teaching and learning the first day of class. And we include the following note in our syllabus:

> *A note on the scholarship of teaching: As professors, we have responsibilities towards advancing "scholarship" in our chosen fields. Recently, we've been defining our area of scholarship as the scholarship of teaching and learning. In particular, we've been thinking about, and writing about, how best to teach so that students become effective, ethical, self-aware participants in the civic lives of their communities. At some point in the future, after the course ends, we might ask to cite some part of your work as evidence in our writing. You would then have the opportunity to deny our request; to allow us to cite your work anonymously; or to allow us to cite your work, with due credit given to you. If in any way this interferes with your ability to learn in this class, please come talk with us, or talk with Dr. Amy Driscoll, CSUMB's Director of Teaching, Learning and Assessment, at 582-4517. In addition, if you'd like to talk with us further about this kind of work—including ways to collaborate, possibly as part of your capstones—please talk with us.*

Then, on the last day of class, we hand out and explain this form:

SBSC/ESSP 385/Fall 2000
Your instructors are engaged in ongoing research to test the effectiveness of their teaching methods. Your written work is some of the best evidence we have of whether or not our teaching is effective.

It is possible that at some point in the future, we will want to use either excerpts of your HIPP project, or your entire HIPP project, as part of articles, portfolios, or presentations we produce. Your written work is your intellectual property, and we cannot use your work without your permission.

Please consider whether or not you are willing to have your work included in future public scholarship. We have assigned a student to collect and hold these forms. We will not look at these forms until after we have submitted our grades for the course.

- ☐ *I do not wish to have my SBSC/ESSP 385 written work used in the scholarly work of Professors Shenk and Takacs.*
- ☐ *I agree to allow Professors Shenk and Takacs to use my SBSC/ESSP 385 written work, but I do not wish to have my name on any quotes they use from my work.*
- ☐ *I agree to allow Professors Shenk and Takacs to use my SBSC/ESSP 385 written work, but they must use my name on any quotes they use from my work.*

If you have any additional concerns or restrictions on how we might use your work, please explain them here:

_____
_____
_____

Please print your name: _____
Please sign your name: _____
Today's date: _____

We ask a student volunteer to collect the forms and give them to us after the course is over and we have submitted our grades. This way, no student feels coerced to participate; they need not fear that their grades will be affected if they decline to give permission. (Of course, if they work with us after the course is over—as advisees, on capstone theses, in other courses—they still may not feel free to withhold permission.)

As our form makes clear, we also give them the right not to have their names used (if they don't want to go public with their values and their views on politics) or to be sure we use their names (if they want credit for the fine work they've produced). We find that most students say they are honored that we might use their work, and want us to use their names.

The one most common concern we hear is that we might use their work in a negative or unflattering light. One student envisioned that we might label his work as "wrong" or "the incorrect way to do things"—accompanied with a kind of game-show music signifying that he is the "weakest link." Of course, there might be times when a scholar of teaching and learning wishes to show examples of great and not-so-great work. But we have resolved that we will never show a student's work as a negative example unless we are showing a before/after comparison of what a given student learned, and unless we have secured his or her permission to do so. What's really at stake here is trust: Students must trust that we will honor them. Will all scholars of teaching and learning do this? Will some simply not consider the consequences of citing a student's less-than-stellar work in public forums?

We faced another dilemma: What happens when we are as transparent as possible in explaining our scholarship of teaching and learning project to students and then, after the class ends, after they've signed the release, we want to make a *different* use of their work than the one originally announced? This happened to us. After we read their final projects, we became interested in a new question—about how students actually used historical knowledge to inform their political projects. We never told them we were going to use their work in this way because we had no idea we would want to. Students had signed releases, and some of them then scattered, as students will do. Meanwhile, we are proceeding with our scholarly project, content that those who have signed releases trust us and that we will maintain that trust by using their work only in the most respectful ways. But this troubles us.

> We would like to take students with us to professional conferences to present their Historically Informed Political Projects and to discuss what they learned about politics and themselves, and how they learned it. Our goal in the scholarship of teaching and learning should be to improve student learning not just for future generations of students; those in our classes now should be benefiting.

The next time we teach the course, our plan is to focus on ways to include students in the scholarship of teaching and learning work. This is also part of a subtle shift in how we've come to think about ethical issues in the scholarship of teaching and learning. We originally had been thinking about what we absolutely have to do to honor ethical commitments to our students and to various institutional functionaries. Now we're thinking about what's the best and most we can possibly do to behave ethically and enhance student learning at the same time. We would like to take a few of our students with us to professional conferences to present their HIPPs and to discuss what they learned about politics and themselves, and how they learned it. Our goal in the scholarship of teaching and learning should be to improve student learning not just for future generations of students; those in our classes now should be benefiting from the work we're doing, should be involved in the work—commenting on it, collaborating on it, framing the questions and answering them.

In short, we want to move from a model of students as subjects to students as collaborators. Understanding how one learns what one learns is a key to lifelong learning. We're looking for a win-win-win situation where we learn as much about teaching effectiveness as possible while simultaneously empowering students present and future to do the best learning possible.

david
TAKACS

Commentary on David Takacs's Case

1 **Amy Driscoll**
Director, Teaching, Learning, and Assessment
California State University, Monterey Bay

David Takacs is already on his way to a resolution in the reflection he includes in the last paragraph. The resolution lies in the alternative to studying our students—that is, collaborating with them for the scholarship of teaching and learning. If we really want students to benefit from our studies of teaching and learning, we need to involve them in the questions that guide our studies, in the design of our inquiry, in the process of collecting data to respond to the questions, and even in the analysis of data for results.

This is a lesson my colleagues and I recently learned in our assessment of community-based learning, or service learning, in the context of community-university partnerships, an area in which I have worked extensively. Using the community as our research sample has been a university tradition, but deeper insights are likely to result when scholars collaborate with members of the community as part of the study process. David's case provides a parallel lesson for the scholarship of teaching and learning. As his report suggests, using students as a research sample may undermine the relationships sought by faculty and by students. Collaboration supports and protects those relationships and, for research purposes, yields broad perspectives, unexpected questions and answers, and rich findings; it's a much better fit for the learning-community culture we seek in our university classes.

At the same time, David's case makes me wonder about faculty assumptions about students' thoughts, fears, perspectives, and needs related to the use of their work. Granted, his assumptions are based on his experiences and interactions with students, but there may be a whole different perspective to be tapped when students collaborate. Their questions may be quite different from ours. We have so much yet to examine in our study of teaching and learning, and students are really the key source of future insights and resulting pedagogy. It's exciting to consider the potential of what we may learn when students become partners in our scholarship of teaching and learning. I can imagine David's class responding in both predictable and interestingly unpredictable ways in this scenario:

Early in the semester, David talks to the class about the scholarship of teaching and learning. He tells them about his praxis pedagogy and the praxis cycle and describes his interest in learning whether it is an effective model for helping the students achieve course outcomes. I can envision a discussion that follows in which students talk about previous learning experiences, preferences for different learning contexts, and how the praxis process fits their learning styles. Eventually David might encourage the class to add some study questions to his major question, Does the praxis cycle of learning experiences support students in achieving the outcomes of … ? Students might ask, Is it different for some of us in how it supports our learning? When the praxis cycle doesn't work, what are the obstacles? After a set of questions is developed, David's class is ready to brainstorm about an appropriate methodology, asking, What can we do to find the answers to these questions?

Through this scenario students are learning experientially about research, about the scholarship of teaching and learning, and, in time, about the ethics of research. In the class context David is modeling collaborative research and the civic engagement about which he is teaching.

Another brief example of this potential occurred on my campus when fifty of our faculty studied the alignment between the learning activities planned for their courses and the outcomes of those courses. In the initial planning we decided that a student voice in the study was as important as a faculty voice for determining whether the activities were aligned with the outcomes. We learned a powerful lesson—that students' perceptions of the alignment frequently differed from the faculty's perceptions. Our data would have looked very different had we included only faculty in the process.

Finally, the circumstance that David describes is a beautiful "teachable moment," especially for a course aimed at helping students become "ethical, effective, self-aware members of communities." Working through the dilemma of how, when, and why students' work is used for data in the study of teaching and learning is ideal both for modeling pedagogy and for learning experientially in the course. For example, as a class project, David's students could develop a class or university policy about using students' work by researching relevant literature, interviewing students and faculty, consulting with the university ombudsperson, or checking with other campuses for policies. Or in small groups, students could work through a set of scenarios that call for ethical decision making.

In sum, I second David's respect for students and his concern about the ethics of using student work for many different purposes. In collaborative classes or learning communities, the decisions David is pondering are best made with students. With guidance, student involvement in decisions about using their work can yield powerful learning for all of us—students and faculty.

CASE 2

Kevin Miller
Student
California State University, Monterey Bay

As a student, I am delighted to see that teachers like David Takacs are trying to see students not as vessels to be filled with information but instead as producers of knowledge. However, I wonder if the teacher's use of student work is sufficiently visible to the students themselves. If I sign a waiver for my own work, and I never see the professor again, how am I to know that my thoughts were used or ignored? Regardless of whether or not my work is used after the semester is over, how does the *eventual* citation of my paper affect my relationship with the professor *during* the semester?

Instead of having the teacher make decisions about the use of student work (which further entrenches the role of the teacher as a justifier of knowledge), students might be encouraged to use one another's work. For instance, I know of one professor who actually requires in a final paper the citation of a peer's work. Whether or not such a requirement is necessary or feasible depends on the nature of the course or assignment; however, the practice can lead to a

> Working through the dilemma of how, when, and why students' work is used for data in the study of teaching and learning is ideal both for modeling pedagogy and for learning experientially. For example, as a class project, David's students could develop a class or university policy about using students' work.

much more cohesive learning community, where each classroom has as many teachers as it does students.

In addition to the issue of student involvement with other students' work, there are two functional problems with asking students to fill out release forms at the end of the semester. First, such forms assume that students can remember all the work they've done in the course and whether they want everything they wrote to be made available. Second, even if students were able to catalog all of their assignments, the all-or-nothing approach does not allow learners to ask that certain papers be used while others are left private. Some of my fellow students said they felt like "gerbils in a cage," that signing the release form allowed for unwarranted criticism and study of their papers. Others didn't even bother reading it before signing, a knee-jerk reaction I can sympathize with in today's educational bureaucracy.

Regardless of the obviously caring motives of the professor, the teacher-student power dynamic still influences whether or not consent is given. In the environment of higher education, traditional classroom relationships are so ingrained in the minds and behaviors of the students that there is a limit to how effective a teacher can be in deconstructing these interactions. To assume that teachers are solely responsible for creating a liberating environment for their students denies the power and agency of the pupils themselves. Students must play an integral role in questioning their relationship with the professor in order for any sort of change in power dynamics to take place. Altering the classroom hierarchy is essential if we are to create an educational paradigm in which students, as actors in the learning process, can excel beyond the expectations of the more traditional teaching and learning environments.

3 Cynthia Scheinberg
English
Mills College

As I sat down to read David Takacs's case about gaining student permission for the scholarship of teaching and learning, I had a number of responses, most circling around "Yes, more of this!" In that wonderful kind of coincidence that often informs my own critical work, next to me was my favorite volume of poems by Adrienne Rich, *Your Native Land, Your Life*, and in it one of my favorite poems about teaching, which seemed oddly suited to the response I was having to David's work.

Rich's poem, "Poetry I," describes students struggling with their learning in traditional ways, "studying the history of poetry" and mastering complex terms like "modernism, trope, vatic, text" (Rich, 1986: 66). Yet, even as they strive to learn the information the academy would have them learn, the students in Rich's poem search urgently for "more"—for "shreds of music," for a link to family history "back in the old country," and, ultimately, for "how to live." In reviewing David's work, I'm struck by the fact that he is finding ways not only to give students that sense of "more," but also to offer "more" to teachers—both in the classroom and in their research. His practical ethic for using student work in the scholarship of teaching and learning thus strikes me as overwhelmingly positive.

For starters, David and his team-teaching colleague Gerald Shenk are making all the right moves and assumptions given our current academic climate. Their efforts to offer students choices in how to be cited, the underlying fear that as professors they will not be trusted in the act of "using" student work, their deep-rooted desire for models of student collaboration—all of their careful reflections and actions demonstrate how deeply they respect their students. Indeed, one suspects that the students themselves must know how much they are respected.

My response to this case is not, however, only about the rightness of the teachers' approach. I also feel sadness about the assumptions that lead to that approach. I hear myself asking: Why must the things David and Gerald are doing with their students seem so complex? Require so much paperwork? Why is the model that they are moving toward—encapsulated in the idea of taking students to conferences with them—still an exception rather than a norm in our academic lives? Why can we not take the concepts of trust, respect, and collaboration for granted in our teaching and our scholarship? And why is it that when we seek to include students in our scholarly work, we are inevitably risking that terrible accusation—from both students and our teaching colleagues—that we are "using" students? Isn't our job to show our students the relevance their own work has for larger teaching, learning, scholarly, and political contexts? Isn't the whole point in higher education to help situate a student's work so that she knows it is not a mere exercise (learning specialized terms like "trope, vatic, text") but rather a kind of work that helps us know, as Rich says, "how to live"—and perhaps how to learn—in the larger and most inclusive sense of the word and world?

Thus, when David writes that "we remain concerned that the prospect of public display might put a chill on that community, preventing our students from investing themselves fully in their work," I find myself coming at the issue from a very different perspective. As when Rich calls for *"More!"* I too want more—more possibility that students will be inspired and engaged in work that is recognized as having public, shared value.

I'm aware (as David is) that the real world poses real risks, that caution is needed. Sometimes student work *is* used inappropriately, and we all know colleagues who truly don't respect their students as individuals. But can we imagine a world of teaching

and learning where our students are by our side at conferences, quoted in our books? Can we imagine a kind of scholarship that takes for granted that our students are important collaborators, rather than a distraction? I'm grateful that David and Gerald are raising ethical issues about our relationships with our students. In so doing, they are clearing paths into a landscape of authentic collaboration with students—paths they make, as Miles Horton would say, simply by walking where they (and we) need to go.

Resources

Ayers, William; Hunt, Jean Ann; and Quinn, Therese. *Teaching for Social Justice.* New York: The New Press, 1998.

Colby, Anne; Ehrlich, Thomas; Beaumont, Elizabeth; and Stephens, Jason. *Educating Citizens: Preparing America's Undergraduates for Lives of Moral and Civic Responsibility.* San Francisco: Jossey-Bass, in press. See Chapter 5, which reports on the course taught by Takacs and Shenk.

Ellsworth, Elizabeth. *Teaching Positions: Difference, Pedagogy, and the Power of Address.* New York: Teachers College Press, 1997.

hooks, bell. *Teaching to Transgress: Education as the Practice of Freedom.* New York: Routledge, 1994.

Maher, Frances A., and Tetrault, Mary Kay Thompson. *The Feminist Classroom.* New York: BasicBooks, 1994.

Rich, Adrienne. *Your Native Land, Your Life.* New York: Norton, 1986.

Shenk, Gerald, and Takacs, David. "History and Civic Participation: An Example of the Scholarship of Teaching and Learning." *Perspectives,* 2000 (April).

Shor, Ira. *When Students Have Power: Negotiating Authority in a Critical Pedagogy.* Chicago: University of Chicago Press, 1996.

Refining Questions and Renegotiating Consent

Suzanne Burgoyne
Theatre
University of Missouri–Columbia

In the fall of 2000 I taught a course on Theatre of the Oppressed (TO), a participatory theatre form developed by Brazilian theorist and director Augusto Boal, building on the liberatory pedagogy of Paolo Freire. Students in the course did several collaborative projects with an education class, and I began work with an interdisciplinary group of four other faculty, representing education, religious studies, counseling psychology, and Black studies, to analyze data from this joint course. Our collaborative study employed both quantitative and qualitative methods: Students from the two classes filled out instruments measuring racial attitudes and completed a survey and journals. After the semester was over the faculty conducted focus groups. We also had participant observer notes and videotapes of the projects. In short, we were generating and collecting a range of different kinds of data. The initial question we wanted to explore was what impact the TO work might have on student attitudes toward race and racial oppression. As the semester unfolded we refined and sharpened that very broad question, and that's where I encountered ethical issues.

Before my team and I collected any data, we went through the campus Institutional Review Board (IRB). I should say that until a few years ago when I started doing qualitative research, I had never heard of an IRB. The kind of research I was used to doing in my field was theatre history and criticism or script analysis; there were no "human subject" issues. But I had a good colleague and mentor working with me when I began doing the scholarship of teaching and learning, and she emphasized very clearly the need to protect students. And

---

Suzanne Burgoyne, a Carnegie Scholar in the class of 2000, is professor of theatre, and vice president for professional development for the Association for Theatre in Higher Education. She has published articles on ethical issues in actor training and directing and is co-author of *Teaching and Performing: Ideas for Energizing Your Classes*.

Respondents

Richard Gale is a faculty member in Theatre and Interdisciplinary Studies with the Hutchins School of Liberal Studies at Sonoma State University. As of July 2002, he is on leave from his campus to work as a senior scholar with the Carnegie/Hewlett Liberal Education Program. He also organizes and facilitates interactive theatre workshops centering on issues of identity, environmental awareness, and racism, and is a member of the board of directors for Pedagogy and Theatre of the Oppressed.

Peter J. Markie is professor of philosophy and vice provost for Undergraduate Studies at the University of Missouri–Columbia. He is author of *A Professor's Duties: Ethical Issues in College Teaching* as well as articles in various areas of philosophy, including ethics and epistemology.

Helen A. Neville teaches in the Counseling Psychology Division and the Afro-American Studies Program at the University of Illinois at Urbana-Champaign. In addition to researching various issues related to racism and mental health, she is interested in examining student learning around diversity issues broadly and also the process through which students develop multicultural competencies.

CASE three

in the TO course project, too, I was glad to have collaborators who were quite experienced with IRB procedures. In any event, it was a given that our work would need to go through that process. It used to be that educational research was exempt on this campus, but that's not true anymore.

Once our research plan was approved by the IRB, the other four faculty and I set about getting consent from the students (each class had an enrollment of fifteen). A third party went into the class to do this; that is, the request for consent didn't come from me, the course instructor. We asked if students would be willing to participate in the research by completing an instrument that measured color-blind attitudes before and after engaging in the TO activities, and by allowing the research team access to the journals they would be keeping as one of the course requirements. Twelve theatre students and thirteen education students gave their approval, but the instructors of the two courses didn't know which students had agreed until the end of the semester, after grades were submitted. (A graduate assistant copied the journals from students who gave their permission to use them for research.)

A significant event happened about a third of the way through the semester: We had a kind of blow-up in the theatre class. We were doing a TO process called Image Theatre. In this process, participants "sculpt" each other into images of an issue they want to explore. For instance, one of the projects my TO class did with the education class was to create images of an "oppressive classroom," then an "ideal classroom"; they then explored ways to move from the oppressive to the ideal. Up to that point in the TO class, we had been playing it safe in our choices of issues to image, so I was urging the students to find an issue with some real meat on it, something we could really explore together. In response, the class proposed several topics, and one thing led to another until the class was split down the middle about whether we should focus on violence or on rape. I didn't want to cast the deciding vote, so one of the students changed his vote—to rape. Our Image Theatre exercise would, then, focus on rape.

Some of the students were extremely uncomfortable with this choice. Ordinarily, in TO work I depend on a rule I call "the right of egress" in order to provide a safety net. That is, students who don't want to participate in a particular exercise can sit out. I thought that rule would work in this situation, too, but the tension in the class was tremendous. Some students chose not to participate, and a couple of them left the room. Others worked on the images. But the whole situation was very tense, and it stayed that way throughout the session.

After the exercise ended, the students and I tried to process what had happened. It became increasingly clear that people were divided about whether we should be dealing with the topic of rape but even, more generally, whether they wanted to deal with what I termed *risky issues*. We discussed what safeguards need to be in place for such work, and what benefits and costs it might have. There was a good deal of hostility. People who were committed to dealing with risky issues felt that they were being restricted by those who didn't want to and vice versa.

Gradually the class worked through all of these concerns, and the semester continued successfully. But I was struck by the experience. It took me pretty much by surprise. This kind of dynamic, where a group splits apart, is not really discussed in the literature on Theatre of the Oppressed. And so, I thought, since we're collecting so much data, it would be especially useful to look at the factors that cause such a situation to occur, the different perspectives on it, how it might be handled, and so forth. My sense that this investigation would be helpful was reinforced when another Carnegie Scholar in theatre—Richard Gale from Sonoma State—told me that he has experienced a similar response teaching TO classes when students weren't sure how far they were willing to go with taking risks.

In short, I saw a chance to contribute to discussion and understanding of the group-dynamic aspect of TO by looking at the student journals with this issue and set of questions in mind. And this was a slightly different, or at least more focused, topic than the research team originally envisioned when we went to the IRB. The procedures the team would follow and our data sources would not change, but our question had shifted a bit. It seems to me this process of refining questions is typical, maybe even inevitable, in the scholarship of teaching and learning. You simply can't know in advance what's going to happen and be significant as a course unfolds.

After the semester ended, the research team sat down and started to code the journals. In doing so we realized that several people had chosen not to participate in the study. And we realized that of the journals we had permission to use, we had more from students who wanted to do the risky work than from those who didn't. So the information was pretty one-sided. Clearly it would be useful to have more journals from students who hadn't wanted to take risks. We talked in our team about whether it would be appropriate to ask some of those students to reconsider, but we all agreed it would be unethical. We had given students the option at the outset, and going back to them now and asking them to reconsider would be a violation of their privacy and autonomy. I had been sensitized to this issue the first time I did a qualitative study because the colleague who was teaching me the methodology made a big point about how careful you need to be if you have any kind of power over potential subjects. Because I'm a teacher, my power continues even after the class. I might be advising students on dissertations, or be asked to write recommendations. If I were to go back and ask students to reconsider, I would be speaking from a position of power, and students might not feel free to say no. So that was the issue. And I feel that we made the right decision about it.

But there was a second ethical issue that emerged, as well. One student initially signed up to be a research participant, but then part way through the semester came to me and said, "I really don't want anybody reading my journal except you." She did not say that she didn't want the journal included in the research, only that she didn't want anyone but me to read it. I agreed, of course, assuring her that no one else on the research team would see it—and in order to ensure her privacy, I didn't give her journal to the graduate

assistant to be copied; so her journal wasn't included in the research materials we were keeping. But because she is a very articulate and insightful student, it occurred to me as she and I were talking that her journal might turn out to contain perspectives that could be significant for our research. So I told her I would not keep a copy of her journal but asked her whether, if at some later time it became apparent that her journal could really contribute to our study, we could discuss the issue again—and she said yes.

Therefore, when my team realized that we had relatively fewer journals on the "nonrisk" side, I considered whether I could approach this student to ask permission to use portions of her journal that would fill out the picture, with the promise that I would be the only member of the team to read and code that particular journal. Meanwhile, in looking back over some of the materials in my private files on the TO course, I found an email from the student in which she was responding to the problematic Image Theatre day. In that missive, she specifically offered me permission to include the email itself in the research project.

Recently, I did indeed talk with the student about using her journal. I was careful to emphasize that she had every right to say no. She readily agreed, however, which I appreciated, but I told her she should continue to think about it and get back to me if she had any second thoughts. A few days later, she sent me her journal. I am the only one from the research team who is reading it, and it does contain significant insights that contribute to our analysis. However, if I want to use any direct quotes from that journal in the article we're writing, I plan to ask the student for permission to use the specific passages. This arrangement seems reasonable to me, but I'm aware that my judgment on this issue is based not only on a general sense of what's ethical but also on a fairly close knowledge of the student. Because of the nature of theatre work, I get to know students quite well. My approach here reflects my sense of her in this specific situation. I wouldn't necessarily want to draw a general principle or rule from this narrative.

> If I want to use any direct quotes from that journal in the article we're writing, I plan to ask the student for permission to use the specific passages. This arrangement seems reasonable to me, but I'm aware that my judgment on this issue is based not only on a general sense of what's ethical but also on a fairly close knowledge of the student.

suzanne BURGOYNE

Commentary on Suzanne Burgoyne's Case

Richard Gale
Theatre Arts and Interdisciplinary Studies
Hutchins School of Liberal Studies
Sonoma State University

This case raises many important issues for the scholarship of teaching and learning, not the least of which is the ethical dilemma surrounding the use of the student journal, which Suzanne Burgoyne discusses at some length. But, for me, the larger question has to do with the nature and level of influence present in a classroom when conflicting agendas are at work. In studying socially laden and emotionally charged learning experiences, does the (admittedly ethical) articulation of a scholarly project change the classroom ecology? Might students' knowledge that their work is being studied discourage some of them from fully engaging (or encourage others to artificially engage) with admittedly risky material? In other words, what interests me in this episode is the ethics of potentially prejudicing student work through the establishment of a research agenda for the class.

This tension is common to much research. How do you avoid influencing the results of an experiment by virtue of the methods you use to gather and analyze data? In a biology experiment, or a clinical drug trial, the answer is in having clear controls. But in the classroom, controls are difficult to establish, and may not yield the most useful data. Furthermore, taking a "control group" approach in an educational setting (especially one so emotionally charged) might compromise or distort the students' experiences by dividing the community. How then do we establish an environment of scholarly rigor while maintaining the integrity of the student experience?

When I read Suzanne's case I was struck by how carefully she followed the IRB procedures, and how diligent she was about ensuring student anonymity, avoiding coerced consent, and providing opportunities for opting out of the analysis. She treats these matters with consummate professionalism. Yet I wonder if the issue of bias, or rather unanticipated influence, persists regardless. After all, these procedures are (rightly) designed to protect the students, not the scholarship.

I experienced a similar problem in undertaking my own scholarship of teaching and learning, which was an examination of portfolio assessment as it relates to student empowerment. One of the most important features of my study was the solicitation of student input regarding the effectiveness and possible revision of an existing portfolio structure. Yet in asking students to volunteer for this activity, I was automatically privileging the voices of those *interested* in change. Similarly, by asking students to opt in or out of a research project associated with Theatre of the Oppressed in the classroom, Suzanne may have been unintentionally influencing the data sample and subtly altering the dynamics of the classroom. This may in turn have contributed to both the "blow-up" in the class and the willingness (or not) to do "risky work." Those already committed to the risk would have no qualms about the study, while those less inclined to take chances would be less inclined to participate.

My reaction here has much to do with my own commitment to Theatre of the Oppressed, a unique process with very specific origins and objectives. It was created out of a need for action, as an opportunity for the silenced to gain a voice, as a way to help the oppressed overcome their oppression. It has since been used in a variety of venues, and to address a much broader spectrum of issues and ideologies. For example, I have used the practice for environmental workshops and conference debriefings, as well as for dealing with difficult pedagogical issues (I am the Carnegie Scholar mentioned by Suzanne in her case). But regardless of the "where" of Theatre of the Oppressed, the "why" remains constant for me: to provide a community with the opportunity to imagine and enact answers to their problems, responses to their circumstances. That was, I believe, what Suzanne had in mind when she created a class in which Theatre of the Oppressed was a primary source of insight and investigation; she gave her students a chance to engage with complex issues in a safe environment. The question is whether, in establishing the class as a site of scholarship at the outset, the purposes of the approach may have been altered or compromised.

One of the things I insist upon when using Theatre of the Oppressed is that there be no observers, no video, no nonparticipants. Because the work involves personal risk and collective trust, it is vital that all those involved share the same level of interaction. I have found that this deepens the level of engagement in the class, and makes the students' experience more personally enriching. However, this approach also makes it more difficult to study the work, for it excludes certain kinds of documentation. Suzanne's use of less intrusive forms of documentation addresses one problem. But there may still be difficulties. By stating at the outset that she was studying the class and intended to use student experience as data, Suzanne certainly ensured a more diverse data set, but she may have skewed the results without realizing it (or even without the students themselves realizing it).

Perhaps what I am suggesting is that such studies, especially those involving very personal circumstances, should be articulated after the fact rather

> What one student actually finds coercive another will not. It is imperative that we monitor our relations with our students and guide our decisions accordingly.

than before. Let the learning and the experience take priority and suggest to the students that, as scholars, they might all investigate the class experience after the community has completed its journey. There have been times, in my own classes, when students have approached me at the end of a course and asked if they could analyze the work of the past semester, and in my own Carnegie work I have provided space and time for this to occur. I can imagine Suzanne approaching her students at the end of this course, suggesting that analysis of the work and the journals would be fruitful, and asking, at that time, for volunteers willing to contribute either their work or their time (or both) to the study. There would still, undoubtedly, be students who opt out, but I wonder if the material collected might not be more revealing and more representative. Of course, this puts an added burden on the scholarship (and on the course-planning apparatus), but it may be a way to provide the researcher with more useful and accurate data, while providing the students with a more authentic experience.

2 Peter J. Markie
Philosophy
University of Missouri–Columbia

Suzanne Burgoyne's case poses several ethical issues. Some concern the appropriate practices for faculty who combine research and teaching, making their class a laboratory and their students research subjects. Others concern the appropriate roles of professors and students in the design and implementation of a course plan. I'll try to identify and sharpen our appreciation of these basic issues, but I certainly won't try to resolve them all.

The most apparent issue with regard to the combination of research and teaching is that of when and how professors should obtain informed consent from their students in order to involve them in research. It is noted in the case that, once upon a time, educational research of the sort involved here was not subject to IRB review and, presumably, was sometimes conducted without the sort of consent procedures now mandated by such review. Does the current system represent an ethical advance? Should such review and consent be required? The main argument for review is based on the institution's responsibility to ensure that its faculty pursue their research in a way that respects human dignity. The main argument for requiring student consent for research activities is based on the fact that (1) we fail to respect individuals' dignity when we involve them in activities without their informed and free consent, (2) the consent students give by simply registering for a course is limited to their participation in activities designed to advance their education, and (3) the research activities, which involve students' essential participation, are designed to advance the instructor's research rather than student education. Thus, the students' additional informed and free consent is required for the research.

Given the necessity for student consent, the case raises the particular issue of what conditions are required for that consent to be uncoerced and therefore free. The relation between students and professors is inherently unequal, given the power that professors have over student education and professional careers. To guard against coercion, consent was initially obtained here in such a way that "the instructors of both classes didn't know which students had agreed until the end of the semester, after grades were submitted." This protects students from any coercion with regard to their course grades, but does it go far enough? The power relationship between instructors and students extends beyond course grades, as Burgoyne notes in explaining why it would be wrong at the end of the course to ask students to reconsider the decision not to participate:

> *Because I'm a teacher, my power continues even after the class. I might be advising students on dissertations, or be asked to write recommendations. If I were to go back and ask students to reconsider, I would be speaking from a position of power, and students might not feel free to say no.*

It is worth considering whether these aspects of the professor-student relationship mandate that the instructors *never* know which students agree to participate and which decline. Just as a student who is asked to reconsider her decision on participation after grades are in might be coerced by the professor's future control over her education and professional career, so too a student who is asked to participate at the start and assured that her decision will only be revealed after grades are in might be coerced by these same aspects of the professor's future power. As the case raises with regard to asking students to reconsider their decisions after the course but overlooks with regard to asking them to participate at the start, the power relation between professors and students can extend far beyond the grade for a particular course. We need to be sensitive to all its aspects.

Awareness of the various aspects of the professor-student relationship and the potential for coercion must be combined with sensitivity to the peculiar dimensions of each case. What one student actually finds coercive another will not. It is imperative that we monitor our relations with our students and guide our decisions accordingly. How then can we tell what a student finds coercive, and what should we do when we cannot be sure? In the case, Burgoyne relies on clear signals from one student that she will not be coerced by a request to reconsider her decision to participate, notes the risk of generalizing this decision to other cases in which such signals may be absent, and opts for a conservative strategy: The presumption to be rebutted is that students will be coerced by a request, not that they won't. Does the presumption always rest with this side or does its location vary with such factors as the sensitivity of the research topic and the nature of the relation between the instructor and the class? Wherever the presumption rests, does the nature of the evidence required to rebut it also vary with such factors?

The case also raises important issues regarding the appropriate roles of professors and students in the design and implementation of course plans. To what extent should a professor determine the plan for a course and present that to students at the start of the semester, thus obtaining their informed consent for the educational activities in which they'll be expected to participate? To what extent may such plans instead be developed as the course moves along, and to what extent may or should the professor involve students in their development? The case reports that a "blow-up" takes place when the instructor, appropriately concerned that the class has been too focused on safe topics, urges the students to pick a less safe one and leaves the determination to them. Their choice leaves some of the class exercising their "right of egress" not to participate, at the cost of foregoing educational opportunities for which they have presumably enrolled in the course, and it leaves the class as a whole tense and very divided. An alternative approach would have been for Burgoyne to share a list of already determined topics, perhaps moving from the safe to the not-so-safe, with the students at the start of the semester. The responsibility for this aspect of the course design would be taken off the students' shoulders, and the topics would be known in advance. Students would be in a position at the start of the semester to determine the commitment involved in participating in the course; their participation would thus be more informed, and divisive blow-ups over subsequent class decisions would be avoided.

These alternative approaches have different implications for student consent and control. The approach taken in the case transfers a degree of responsibility for course planning to the students as a class. It supports their autonomy as a group by allowing them to decide on the topics of study. Yet, in supporting their autonomy as a group, it restricts their autonomy as individuals. Each particular student's decision to participate in the class at the start of the semester is less informed than it would be if the topics were determined in advance. Some students, having decided to participate in the class, are later faced with the surprise choice between participating in an activity they find uncomfortable or foregoing that part of the course. Presumably, at this point in the semester, the option of taking a different course entirely is no longer available. The alternative plan more fully supports the autonomy of each individual student. At the start of the semester, each decides to participate in the course and makes the decision on the basis of a detailed plan of the topics to be covered. It does not, however, involve the students as a class in the course design. That activity is taken over by the professor. The students, as a class, do not exercise their autonomy by determining the design of their own course of study.

A comparison of the research and teaching dimensions is tempting here, given that each involves issues of informed consent. In research, we are, unquestionably, concerned with honoring the individual autonomy of each subject. The research design is planned by the researcher, not by the subjects as a group. The design is communicated to subjects at the start of the activity; each gives his or her informed consent to participate in accord with that design. We don't concern ourselves with promoting group autonomy by having research subjects determine the details of the study as it goes along. Should we take the same approach in instruction? If we do, we'll take the second approach just outlined. That is, the topics for study will be determined by the instructor and communicated to the students, who will each decide about participating. Again, the focus remains on promoting the autonomy of each individual student, rather than on fostering the autonomy of the class by having it determine topics. Are the research and instruction cases so analogous that the approach proper to the former carries over in this way to the latter? What is the proper balance

> An intuitively appealing principle is that the class is a class first and a research laboratory second; the students are students first and research subjects second. Under this view, any change in course design or content to promote a research goal should be subject to the condition that it at least not detract from the educational value of the course.

between an instructor's desire to involve the class in the design of her course and a student's need to have a clear design to which to consent in advance?

While the issue of informed consent runs through both the research and instructional issues of the case, additional issues concern the professional responsibility of instructors. Whenever teaching and research are combined, there's the issue of how far a professor may go in modifying course goals or content to serve the demands of the research project. In the case, the research was based on a broad question that was refined as the semester unfolded, and that refining of the research question provided the occasion for the ethical issues. To what extent was the instructor's desire for the class to consider "less safe" issues determined by a sense of what was best for the research project? To what extent was it determined by a sense of what was best for the class? To what extent might those two perspectives have conflicted? They need not always conflict. Yet the question remains of which perspective has primacy in determining the course content. An intuitively appealing principle is that the class is a class first and a research laboratory second; the students are students first and research subjects second. Under this view, any change in course design or content to promote a research goal should be subject to the condition that it at least not detract from the educational value of the course. Yet, even with this principle in hand, we face the difficult question of how we are to determine whether changes will promote research goals at the expense of instruction, as well as how we are to guard against letting research ambitions color our instructional judgment. The former requires a clear sense of the course's instructional goals; the latter, a clear sense of what we are about in our professional roles. Once again, and not surprisingly, resolving ethical issues in teaching and the scholarship of teaching demands a developed sense of what we are about both as teachers and as professionals.

3. Helen A. Neville
Educational Psychology and Afro-American Studies and Research Program
University of Illinois at Urbana-Champaign

The dilemmas outlined by Suzanne Burgoyne in the description of her Theatre of the Oppressed research project underscore the complexity of ethical issues involved in the scholarship of teaching. I was captivated by her summary. It addresses many important issues related to teaching and learning about diversity and oppression: establishing confidentiality, creating a safe yet challenging environment, balancing between process and content, and allaying student fears that they are being evaluated according to the professor's values. My comments below focus especially on the ethical dimensions of these issues.

My observations are based on my reading of Burgoyne's case but also on my role as a member of the research team. I was an active participant in the project's design and data-collection phases. Later in the process, I moved to another educational institution; as a result I have not been as active in the data-analysis phase. My comments center on two main dilemmas raised in the vignette: (a) issues involved when the research questions are altered after the commencement of the project and (b) issues related to voluntary participation.

Teaching and learning is a dynamic process. Although we create syllabi to structure the classroom experience, each time we teach the course, it's different. Classes have their own "personalities," there are differences in reactions to lectures and class exercises, external events may impact class content and process (e.g., September 11, 2001), etc. On the one hand, the dynamic nature of our courses is what makes teaching exciting. Conversely, though, it can create hurdles in our lives as researchers of teaching. Unless we adopt a strict pre- and post-test design in which students complete a structured survey at the beginning and end of the semester, our efforts to assess the effects of instruction on student learning will take a less than predictable path. Moreover, pre- and post-test designs may help to gather information about the general impact of the class experience (for example, whether or not the Theatre of the Oppressed experience increased students' awareness of racial oppression), but this type of design provides little in terms of understanding the *process* through which learning occurs—what students found helpful or hindering and how they responded to specific class experiences. When one is interested in the *process of learning*, qualitative or open-ended data are more appropriate. And in qualitative research, questions are very likely—as in Burgoyne's case—to evolve and shift as the semester progresses.

The dilemma then becomes what to do when the research questions change midstream. There are a number of options. One option is to couch the project in very vague terms (e.g., "we are interested in understanding students' reactions to the course over time") when first seeking approval through the Institutional Review Board. By framing the research project as broadly as possible researchers are given latitude to shape and reshape the focal questions. But because students sign a consent form outlining the extent of participation, and the particular methods of data collection, there is less latitude in terms of process. Thus, when an interesting class dynamic emerges that warrants more focused investigation, researchers have to "hope and pray" that students comment on this in the agreed upon assignments

that have been approved as part of the research design (e.g., journals, reaction papers, etc.).

Another approach is to seek consent for more than one project. In Burgoyne's case, the researchers could have conducted a separate inquiry on the "blow up" or critical incident. It might, for instance, have been possible to obtain a separate human subjects approval to investigate students' reactions to the specific event via an anonymous in-class reaction paper, focus group discussion, individual interview, etc. Naturally, consent for participation in this aspect of the project would be sought when the instructor was not present, and students would be assured that participation would be confidential and voluntary. The advantage of this approach is that the researchers would be able to obtain in-depth information about the incident of interest. The disadvantage is that one might receive information only from those people who feel safe enough to respond. To offset the potential for selection bias, it may be important to collect strictly confidential information for the ministudy (i.e., names or code numbers would be attached to the data that participants contribute).

Designing a separate ministudy does not fully address the question of what to do when students decide to withdraw their participation from the investigation altogether. Although students are given consent forms to keep for their records, there is no guarantee that they will, in fact, keep the forms. Students thus may not know whom to contact if they want to withdraw their participation. In the case, the student felt comfortable sharing her misgivings with Burgoyne. But not all teachers have established such a strong relationship and trust with their students. In these instances, what recourse do students have? For ethical reasons, it is critical that students know how to contact the director of the research project, so that they can withdraw their participation at any time. This can be done by including the information on the syllabus.

To help students understand the teacher vs. researcher distinction, it may be useful to establish a contingency protocol in advance. One aspect of this might be to identify a "point person" to whom all issues would be referred. Had this approach been used, Burgoyne would have been able to respond to the concerned student in her role as teacher, not as researcher, referring the student to the team's point person—who would then consult with the student about her concerns and determine whether or not the student would like to withdraw from the study.

I have saved the most complicated set of issues for last: how to ensure voluntary, noncoercive participation. This typically is not a problem when one is collecting completely anonymous information, as in the case of surveys or short, open-ended responses, where the instructor would have no way of knowing who agreed to participate in the study, and who did

> To help students understand the teacher vs. researcher distinction, it may be useful to establish a contingency protocol in advance. One aspect of this might be to identify a "point person" to whom all issues would be referred.

not. The problem arises when more extensive data like journals and other narratives are included. Many faculty will be able to identify their students by their writing style or content. The problem with being able to "guess" whose voice is present is that one can also figure out whose voice is missing and thus who decided not to participate in the study. Many students know this and may feel a bit coerced into participating. Some students may worry that the faculty member will "find out" that they decided not to participate in the study and that this will put them at risk in a subsequent course or other evaluative situation. In such a situation, assuring students that faculty will not know who participated in the study until after the grades are turned in is of little comfort. It may, therefore, be important to find ways to ensure that faculty will never be informed about students' participation status. Perhaps other members of the research team—and not the instructor—could complete the textual analyses of the written work.

In sum, Burgoyne's thoughtful case is complex and nuanced, addressing a number of critical dilemmas related to the scholarship of teaching. It appears she handled the major dilemmas introduced in the case in an ethical and reasonable manner. However, her case raises broader concerns about obtaining informed consent when the direction of the research project shifts and about ensuring truly voluntary participation in research on teaching. As suggested in my comments above, I believe that one part of the solution to these and other ethical dilemmas is that the teacher-researcher work with a *team*. A research team can assist in data collection and analyses and help ensure student confidentiality and anonymity as well as voluntary participation.

Resources

Bersoff, D. N. (ed.). *Ethical Conflicts in Psychology.* 2nd Ed. Washington, D.C.: American Psychological Association, 1999.

Boal, Augusto. *Games for Actors and Non-Actors.* (Adrian Jackson, trans.) London: Routledge, 1992.

Cahn, Steven M. *Saints and Scamps: Ethics in Academia.* Totowa, N.J.: Rowman and Littlefield, 1986.

Kincheloe, Joe L., and Steinberg, Shirley R. *Unauthorized Methods: Strategies for Critical Teaching.* New York: Routledge, 1998.

Markie, Peter J. *A Professor's Duties.* Totowa, N.J.: Rowman and Littlefield, 1994.

Schutzman, Mady, and Cohen-Cruz, Jan (eds.). *Playing Boal: Theatre, Therapy, Activism.* New York: Routledge, 1993.

Shor, Ira. *Empowering Education: Critical Teaching for Social Change.* Chicago: University of Chicago Press, 1992.

Strike, Kenneth. *Liberty and Learning.* New York: St. Martin's Press, 1982.

CASE four

Balancing Pedagogic Needs with the Needs of a Classroom Experiment

Charles McDowell
Computer Science
University of California, Santa Cruz

During the 2000-2001 academic year I was co–primary investigator on a National Science Foundation–supported teaching study that involved the use of a classroom comparison group. The other investigators and I were looking at the use of "pair programming" in our beginning programming class for computer science and computer engineering majors. In pair programming, the students work in two-person teams on the programming assignments. Unlike typical "programming-project" classes, where each student is responsible for a different part of the project, with pair programming two students work side-by-side at a single computer. One student is the driver, controlling the mouse and keyboard, and the other student is the reviewer. Pair programming requires that the students periodically switch roles, spending roughly equal amounts of time in each role. This style of programming is being used successfully in industry, producing programs with fewer errors for about the same programmer cost. We wanted to see if pair programming could be used effectively in an educational setting. In particular, we wanted to know how pair programming would affect student performance, student enjoyment, and student perception of computer science as a discipline.

For obvious reasons it was not possible to perform a blind study. The students would easily be able to figure out that in one class work was done in pairs while in the other assignments were to be done independently. In addition, we were not comfortable with randomly assigning students in a single class into two groups, one group that used pair programming and one group that did not. It seemed to us that in such a

---

Charles McDowell is professor of computer science at the University of California, Santa Cruz, where he recently received an Excellence in Teaching Award. A 2001 Carnegie Scholar, his research interests include how to improve the teaching of programming-related topics in computer science. He is co-author of a computer programming textbook.

Respondents

Peter Alexander's interests include developmental mathematics for traditionally underserved populations and the role of undergraduate mathematics in helping students become active citizens. At Heritage College, he has developed a course for preservice teachers entitled Math and Social Justice, which was a context for his work as a 1999 Carnegie Scholar.

Heather Bullock is assistant professor of psychology at the University of California, Santa Cruz, where she teaches courses on poverty, social class, and economic justice. She is interested in active approaches to teaching and learning including service learning and other types of community-based educational experiences.

Eileen Tanner specializes in faculty development for teaching in the research university. As director of the Center for Teaching Excellence at UC Santa Cruz, she supported faculty efforts to contribute to the emerging scholarship of teaching and learning. She is now affiliated with the University of Illinois, Chicago.

CASE four

scenario students who were required to work alone would complain that they were being graded in the same way as students who were allowed to work in pairs. Instead, we decided to teach the class one quarter using pair programming and in a different term teach the class without using pair programming. In order to make the classes as similar as possible, the same instructor, namely me, taught both offerings of the course. Additionally, we collected data on two more offerings of the course during the winter term. Different instructors taught the winter courses.

During the final quarter of data collection, I was teaching the comparison class. This was my second offering of the course during the academic year, and it was the course in which I required students to complete the programming assignments individually as we had always done in the past. This was a rather large class with an enrollment of about 130 students. Part way through the class I became concerned about classroom attendance and the general failure of the students to read the textbook prior to coming to class. This was not a new problem; I've experienced it many times before. In the past I have often considered using short unannounced quizzes to get the students to read the text before I cover the material in class. However, I had rejected this approach because I like to think that the students are adults, and I do not want to treat them like high-school students. I rejected this technique despite the fact that it was used by professors in my classes when I was an undergraduate. Last spring, I felt I had finally reached the point where I was ready to try the pop-quiz technique. However, because the class was part of an ongoing study, I ultimately decided not to use pop quizzes. The ethical question I faced in this decision is about competing goods: At what point do the immediate benefits of changing a classroom technique outweigh the long-term benefits that might be derived from more closely controlling the experiment? This is a difficult question because it was not a matter of deciding whether or not to use a technique that I was certain would help the class. I don't actually know that student learning and performance would have increased significantly had I started using pop quizzes.

> In the past I have often considered using short unannounced quizzes to get the students to read the text before I cover the material in class....However, because the class was part of an ongoing study, I ultimately decided not to use pop quizzes. The ethical question I faced in this decision is about competing goods: At what point do the immediate benefits of changing a classroom technique outweigh the long-term benefits that might be derived from more closely controlling the experiment?

The control group presented a second ethical dilemma. During the fall term in which pair programming was used, we asked the students to submit a log of the time they spent working on the program. This data was important for our study (we wanted to know how long they spent completing the assignments), but it also had a pedagogical value. As their teacher, I needed to make sure that students were actually following the rules of pair programming. This requires that they each spend roughly equal amounts of time "driving" and "reviewing." The log was my mechanism for (a) reminding the students each week about the need to balance their time driving and reviewing, and (b) monitoring how they were actually spending their time so that I could intervene if necessary. The ethical problem was that, in the spring term when students were not working in pairs, I still needed to find out how much time they spent working on the programs. However, there was no pedagogical reason for me to collect this data. Although small, this was extra work that I simply had to insist that they do. Looking back I suppose one option would have been to offer some small payment for completion of the logs. Should I have paid both groups? Are there other options? Given that it was only a few minutes per week, was it reasonable simply to insist they complete the log, in the "interest of science and society"?

CASE four

Commentary on Charles McDowell's Case

1

Peter Alexander
Mathematics
Heritage College

Among the ethical dilemmas raised here are two that occur frequently in the scholarship of teaching and learning: (1) experimental rigor versus best interests of the subjects, and (2) burdening students for the sake of the experiment.

The researcher made a judgment call, as we all must in these situations, weighing possible increased benefit to the subjects versus reduced rigor of the experiment. Pop quizzes would have introduced a confounding variable between the treatment and control groups. Perhaps one could step back and ask if the experiment could be enhanced by introducing pop quizzes. Maybe the experiment had gone far enough to provide a comparison between pair and individual programming. In this case adding quizzes might allow a sub-experiment, comparing pair programming with individual programming-plus-quizzes. The two key points are: (1) Experimental rigor will never be high when comparing actual classroom situations, and (2) I think we must err in the direction of supporting student learning even if it might reduce the quality of the data. That said, I am not a fan of pop quizzes.

Data on student learning are at the heart of the scholarship of teaching and learning. Though much of the data—such as student papers, Web sites, and threaded discussions—arises naturally, sometimes scholars of teaching and learning need additional data, such as student demographic data, that are not directly related to student learning. McDowell's concern about imposing additional work on students is an important one. However, I think there often may be a win-win solution. In this case, data gathering can be designed so students are encouraged to reflect upon their own learning—to become co-reflectors with the teacher on the process of learning. Student journals often serve this function, but they require considerable student and instructor time. Another approach, more narrowly focused on study time, would be for McDowell's students to record not only the time spent programming but also the quality of that time. Such an approach might contribute to student learning as well as provide additional research data. Students could be provided with a rubric or, better, participate in the rubric design (see accompanying example).

Quality of Study Time for a Programming Class
(Partial Rubric)

Task	Excellent	Adequate	Inadequate
Understand the problem			
Design program	Define the key data structures and the functions to be performed by the key submodules. Design the control structures and diagram the flow of data and processing.	Identify the key data structures and submodules	Give names to the subprocesses
Write code			
Test and debug			
Document			

A rubric like this could help students to understand performance criteria for the fundamentals of "good industry practice," and, as a consequence, to use their study time more effectively. Students would be expected to log their daily study time, estimate the approximate fraction of time spent on each programming activity, and assess the quality of their study time. For example, for a given date the student's log might read: "Study time 90 minutes. 40% writing code (Adequate), 30% testing and debugging (Excellent), 30% fooling around on the computer." Recording this information would not be time consuming and would encourage students to reflect on their activities. The data could be graphed, displaying visually the task, study time, and quality for each day of the project. A student's programming process could then be correlated with her performance. As an added benefit in the case of programming, the graphs may illuminate for students the cyclical nature of understanding the problem, designing, coding, and debugging.

2

Heather E. Bullock
Psychology
University of California, Santa Cruz

This case poses two related ethical questions concerning the nature of learning and the choices faculty make about the use of classroom and student time. However, the overarching theme is the tension around the intersections of teaching and research. Teaching is typically characterized as a relatively "selfless" endeavor; though faculty experience numerous rewards from teaching, these "rewards" generally do not guide how we structure our courses. Readings are selected and assignments are designed to optimize student learning and mastery of the course material.

Conducting research that involves students, particularly in our own classroom, sets up parallel and, at times, competing objectives and considerations. Rather than giving assignments based solely on their pedagogical merit, other considerations more closely rooted in research design and methodology may influence our decisions. McDowell's discussion of requiring students in the control group to complete programming logs epitomizes this type of ethical friction. The underlying assumption is that requiring research participation, particularly when there is no overt benefit to the individual student, creates a dilemma in which the ethics of teaching conflict with the demands of research. McDowell describes this tension as being greatest for the control group, whose members weren't given the opportunity to reap the

> McDowell's concern about imposing additional work on students is an important one. However, I think there often may be a win-win solution. In this case, data gathering can be designed so students are encouraged to reflect upon their own learning—to become co-reflectors with the teacher on the process of learning.

potential benefits of the treatment (e.g., pair programming) but were still required to complete brief logs documenting their work. To justify this assignment, he questions whether paying students would have been a fairer way to handle the situation, hence providing them with at least some tangible compensation for their time.

I would like to offer an alternative perspective that minimizes this conflict. Research participants, even those in the control group, may benefit in subtle, indirect ways that might not be anticipated or predicted from a strictly pedagogical perspective. In this case, the control group may have gained knowledge about their work habits by completing self-reflective logs tracking the amount of time spent on assignments. In fact, what superficially appears to be participation in research in the "interest of science and society" may ultimately be a valuable learning experience for students themselves. Participating in research can teach students to critically evaluate scientific findings, help them gain a firmer understanding of research methodology, and encourage their identification as members of an academic community in which both students and faculty actively seek knowledge. Offering monetary compensation may undermine the potential for learning by leading students to think about their participation as financially driven ("I did it for the money"), rather than as a meaningful intellectual activity.

As McDowell points out, we don't always know which techniques will work well in the classroom—whether it is a matter of giving pop quizzes, dropping a particular reading from the curriculum, or trying a new approach in one course but not another. But when a decision appears more closely tied to research than to pedagogy, we may find ourselves questioning these choices, worrying that they advance science over learning. This conflict may be largely resolved when research is constructed as a broader learning experience (not as a source of immediate personal gain), both for faculty and students.

3

Eileen M. Tanner
Director, Center for Teaching Excellence
University of California, Santa Cruz

In his third paragraph Charlie McDowell describes an instructional challenge that he (and legions of other faculty) experience commonly: Students are not all coming to class regularly or are not coming prepared for the particular lesson. He is tempted to try a technique that his professors used when he was an undergraduate, namely pop quizzes. Presumably students would be more inclined to show up, and be prepared to learn, if they knew that their quiz results would be figured into their final grades for the course. The instructor's dilemma in this situation takes on greater significance because he is conducting a formal experiment in the scholarship of teaching and learning by comparing two different approaches to teaching programming. He opts against the pop-quiz solution to maintain the purity of the experiment but wonders whether the immediate benefits of changing a classroom technique should have outweighed the long-term benefits of closely controlling the experiment.

The crux of Charlie's instructional quandary is the point where two sets of objectives, the instructional and the experimental, seem to run orthogonally to one another, and it is from there that ethical questions start to emerge. As an instructor dedicated to his students and their learning, what, if any, professional responsibility does Charlie have in this situation? The pop quizzes represent a teaching tool, a means to shape student behavior, ideally producing a positive effect on learning in the course and with additional potential to affect attendance and preparation. Yet pop quizzes also have potentially negative effects: Charlie has rejected the technique in the past because he wants to treat his students as adults. Presumably he does not want to give students the impression that they are not fully capable of tak-

> We don't always know which techniques will work well in the classroom—whether it is a matter of giving pop quizzes, dropping a particular reading from the curriculum, or trying a new approach in one course but not another. But when a decision appears more closely tied to research than to pedagogy, we may find ourselves questioning these choices, worrying that they advance science over learning.

ing responsibility for their attendance and course preparation. Perhaps he remembers less than favorably what it felt like in courses where his instructors gave pop quizzes. Moreover, he acknowledges not knowing whether this teaching tool will have the desired effects.

In light of these uncertainties, is it acceptable for him simply to teach as he was taught, incorporating short unannounced quizzes to motivate student attendance and readiness for learning in this course? Or should Charlie delve into the educational literature to uncover what others may have already demonstrated about the effectiveness (or lack of effectiveness) of pop quizzes in accomplishing his particular objectives? Might he even have an obligation to his students to do so?

Intersecting with this instructional uncertainty is the experiment itself with its set of requirements. As a computer scientist investigating an aspect of his own teaching, Charlie is seeking to make the two offerings of the course as similar as possible for purposes of comparison and analysis. Was it a good decision, for the sake of the experiment, to overlook the problems of poor attendance and lack of readiness for learning?

A possible solution to this dilemma may lie at this intersection. Charlie's uncertainty occurs in the class where students are working on their programming assignments individually, as opposed to in pairs. Did he find students similarly unprepared to learn in the class where students worked together on their assignments? If not (and he does not mention having faced the same issue in that class), might the pair-programming approach affect student attendance and preparation? Perhaps there is an opportunity here to enlarge the experiment to address this question. The first step would be to articulate his definition of student performance so that it encompasses both attendance and preparation for learning. Charlie could then begin to look at those aspects of the learning experience. He would have a context for reviewing the educational literature to uncover what is already known about pop quizzes, as well as about attendance and readiness for learning. From his investigations new contributions to the scholarship of teaching and learning would potentially emerge.

Resources

Bell, J. T. "Anonymous Quizzes: An Effective Feedback Mechanism." *Chemical Engineering Education,* 1997, 31, 56–57.

Chastain, G., and Landrum, E. (eds.). *Protecting Human Subjects: Departmental Subject Pools and Institutional Review Boards.* Washington, D.C.: American Psychological Association, 1999.

Elton, Lewis. "Strategies to Enhance Student Motivation: A Conceptual Analysis." *Studies in Higher Education,* 1996, 21(1), 57–68.

Kerkman, D. D.; Kellison, K. L.; Piñon, M. F.; Schmidt, D.; and Lewis, S. "The Quiz Game: Writing and Explaining Questions Improve Quiz Scores." *Teaching of Psychology,* 1994, 21, 104–106.

Williams, Laurie, and Kessler, Robert R. "All I Really Need to Know About Pair Programming I Learned in Kindergarten." *Communications of the ACM,* 2000 (May).

———. "Experimenting with Industry's 'Pair-Programming' Model in the Computer Science Classroom." *Journal on SW Engineering Education,* 2000 (Dec.).

CASE five

Too Close for Comfort and/or Validity?

Tomás Galguera
Education
Mills College

I have often informed my decisions concerning ethical research issues by considering the nature of the relationship that I have with the people involved in my research. At one extreme, this relationship may be quite distant and impersonal, as is generally the case with large-scale survey research. The ethical issues that emerge from this type of research tend to be relatively uncomplicated, especially since the researcher's influence over the informants is limited. In most cases, informants have total control over the research medium and conditions, and removing themselves from the study is as easy as not completing a questionnaire, hanging up a telephone, or walking away. The ethical issues in experimental and quasi-experimental research tend to be a bit more complicated. Experiments are about the purposeful manipulation by the researcher of the conditions under which data are collected. Furthermore, subjects participating in experiments often receive compensation, which adds yet another layer of potential ethical problems. The status and power differences between the researcher and the subjects in this and other research traditions create the need for a system of checks and balances in the form of institutional research review committees.

In contrast with experimental research, some of us engage in demographic and phenomenological inquiry in which our relationships with those we study go beyond what is detailed in the study's protocol. Ethical questions in experimental research are typically defined by procedures, but they may explode into ethical tangles and dilemmas when relationships between the researcher and informants or other participants in the study are both long lasting and relatively close. This is particularly so in teaching, an enterprise that is

---

Tomás Galguera is assistant professor in the Teachers for Tomorrow's Schools teacher education program at Mills College in Oakland, California. His teaching, research interests, and publications focus on the preparation of teachers for language-minority students. In 2001 he was named a Carnegie Scholar.

Respondents

Camille Calica is a Spanish bilingual kindergarten teacher in Hayward, California. She is a member of a teacher-researcher group at her school, supported by a grant from the Spencer Foundation. She is currently working toward a master's degree in education at Mills College.

David Donahue is assistant professor of education at Mills College and co-director of the English and social studies teacher credential program. Areas of interest include teacher learning, English and social studies education, education for justice, and human rights.

Judith Haymore Sandholtz is assistant professor in the Graduate School of Education at the University of California, Riverside, where she directed the Comprehensive Teacher Education Institute. Her research focuses on teachers' professional development. As a 2001 Carnegie Scholar, she is examining how beginning teachers learn to analyze their own teaching.

CASE five

fundamentally moral (Soltis, 1990). Especially in researching one's own teaching practice in ways that include students and their work, it is impossible to separate the research from the relationships. This is particularly the case when collegiality is the norm and the effectiveness of teaching depends on one's ability to develop close relationships with students. As a teacher educator in a program that makes collegiality one of its explicit norms, this is my current situation.

The ethical issues in research involving people who share relationships that go beyond that of "researcher" and "subject" or "informant" have multiple facets. In this sense, the phrase *ethical issues* may refer to norms, rules, and standards—the "ethic" of the educational research community. As a member of this community, I have to question the reliability and validity of the findings from research involving individuals with whom I have established relationships. Because of the high probability of researcher bias and socially desirable responses, I can imagine seasoned researchers advising anyone against engaging in research of this kind. Yet, especially in a field such as education, in which the complexity of phenomena often spills out of the best research designs, an in-depth knowledge of the individuals and context of the phenomenon in question may in fact offer greater explanatory potential.

> I have to question the reliability and validity of the findings from research involving individuals with whom I have established relationships. Yet, especially in a field such as education, in which the complexity of phenomena often spills out of the best research designs, an in-depth knowledge of the individuals and context may in fact offer greater explanatory potential.

A related set of ethical issues revolves around the relationships that the researcher has with the people participating in the study. In this case, the code or "rules of good conduct" are not restricted to the educational research community. Rather, the "ethic" is that of our culture and society at large. Ethical boundaries in relationships between people often gain in clarity and definition with time and degree of closeness. Ironically, older, stronger relationships among people also tend to allow for greater flexibility of acceptable behavior among acquaintances. ("Friends will accept you no matter what.") Furthermore, the ethics of relationships are idiosyncratic and culturally dependent. How far individuals will go to assist acquaintances and which costs are acceptable to sustain a relationship are by no means universal limits. The wide diversity of cultures present in most educational settings, especially in California where my work is situated, requires us to consider these questions carefully.

The ethical issues that I want to focus on here emerge out of such a context. My current research consists of a case study based on one of my former students, Camila Calica, a Latina elementary school teacher who has since become a colleague, a mentee, and a friend. (I had to pause and think about whether to write a pseudonym or her real name. I decided on the latter after imagining what Camila would have said had I asked her—and also because she agreed to be a respondent to this case.) I am interested in finding out what

the learning-to-teach process is like for future Latino teachers. Although the question behind the study is one that I have considered for quite some time, the impetus behind this research project stemmed from pressure to "produce scholarly work" associated with my pretenure review.

I had spoken with Camila about my interest in learning more about her development as a teacher while she was a student in the program. I was aware that she had her own questions and concerns regarding her culture, ethnicity, and bilingualism and the role that these had in her teaching. She and I were two of a handful of Latino students and faculty at Mills College when she began her studies two years ago. Though Camila was born in the United States and her father is of Filipino descent, she identifies herself as Latina and is quite proficient in oral Spanish. Besides culture and language, Camila and I shared a belief in bilingual education and the importance of teaching students in culturally congruent ways. While she was a student in the program, I was Camila's professor and student-teacher supervisor. Thus, I observed her teach almost every other week. Lengthy debriefing sessions often followed my observations. We also exchanged countless email messages and talked either in person or over the telephone throughout the academic year. Toward the end of the spring semester, when she began searching for a job among the local districts, I helped Camila sort through the various employment options that were available to her.

Thus it should not be surprising that, at the beginning of the summer, when I began pondering possible studies to submit as proposals for the annual American Educational Research Association (AERA) meeting, I thought of a case study based on Camila. After all, I had considerable data in the form of assignments, evaluation forms, emails, and notes about our conversations. The time was also right to contribute to a growing discussion within the educational research community about teacher diversity—or the lack thereof—and its educational implications.[1] When I approached Camila with this idea, she was quite enthusiastic about the study. We even talked about the possibility of a joint presentation and eventual joint authorship on the research report. In the end, Camila felt intimidated by the prospect of preparing for a presentation while in her first year as a teacher and chose not to be a co-presenter. Still, we both agreed that there was a great need to learn more about how Latino teachers become teachers.

Writing the AERA proposal helped me clarify the conceptual framework behind the study. The process was also helpful in focusing the question on issues of ethnicity and professional and personal self-schemas. Because of this and because of the nature of the data I had already available, I chose to carry out the study informed by the literature on narrative research methodology (Clandinin and Connelly, 2000). The proposal I submitted described a list of preliminary results, which represented conclusions that I had reached after thinking about what I had learned from Camila and reviewing pertinent literature. Our busy schedules limited our discussion of research outcomes and conclusions to email exchanges. Still, she was instrumental in my decision to assign a central function to her narratives. Though we did not find out that my proposal had been accepted until after the new school year had begun, Camila and I met during the summer. We

---

1   See June A. Gordon's (2000) *The Color of Teaching* for a review of the literature on this topic. This is a comparative case study of African American, Latino, Native American, and Asian American teachers that examines the relevance of race and ethnicity in teaching.

five CASE

talked about what we had been doing since the end of the school year, which for me included preparing my pretenure review dossier and materials for my fall semester courses. Camila had been teaching summer school and getting ready to teach in a Spanish-bilingual kindergarten classroom. She was somewhat concerned by this prospect.

As it turned out, Camila was quite comfortable in sharing with me both riveting and enlightening stories about her family and herself. Our data-gathering sessions were never interviews. Rather, they were conversations in which we both explored our experiences as students, teachers, and, now, researchers. In addition, I visited Camila's Spanish-bilingual kindergarten classroom on a regular basis. As we used to do when Camila was student-teaching, we followed my visits with debriefing sessions. During these debriefing sessions, as well as in most of our meetings, we would often cover a wide range of issues, crossing professional, political, social, and personal boundaries. The research protocol that we followed consisted mostly of making sure that we "stayed on track," that we came back to issues of culture, ethnicity, and language, and that we articulated for each other any of our conclusions. The nature of our conversations made it easy for me to tell Camila about my own experiences as a Latino gaining a foothold in an academic community that often felt and made me feel foreign.

> I am troubled by possible challenges to the reliability and validity of my findings, particularly since I cannot claim to be objective toward Camila. I have strived, however, to be objective about conclusions and claims that I make regarding the learning-to-teach process for Latina beginner teachers.

As I sit down to write this reflection on my scholarship of teaching, I think about needing to edit and revise the draft of Camila's case study before she returns from a much-anticipated trip to México. I am curious about what Camila learned about México and herself and impatient to hear her stories about the trip. I am also curious and a bit concerned about what she will think about the case study, not so much about whether I "got it right," but about whether my conclusions resonate with her experience as a beginning Latina teacher.[2]

I began this introspection by considering the ethical issues that arise from research of the kind that I find most valuable at my present state of development as an educator and a scholar. Though this does not reflect the chronology of the process, I will examine these issues in the context of my research and relationship with Camila. I am troubled by possible challenges to the reliability and validity of my findings, particularly since I cannot claim to be objective toward Camila. I have strived, however, to be objective about conclusions and claims that I make regarding the learning-to-teach process for Latina beginner teachers. On the one hand, I wish there were more Camilas who want to become teachers not only in our program but also in the state and the nation. I believe there is a moral obligation on my part and that of fellow teacher educators to

---

2 See Robert K. Yin's (1994) *Case Study Research: Design and Methods* for a thorough description of case study research methods, including the importance of participant and informant comments on report drafts as well as pertinent ethical issues.

prepare teachers with cultural, ethnic, and linguistic backgrounds similar to those of their students. On the other hand, I realize that background similarities between teachers and students do not guarantee ideal educational outcomes.

My ethical mandate as a researcher, then, is to report my findings, even when those findings suggest that there may be no differences in the way in which Latina and White teachers develop, which might undermine arguments for greater teacher diversity (Gordon, 2000). Furthermore, it is my ethical responsibility as a researcher to make sure that I test all other possible explanations, *especially* when my findings support my political and moral convictions. I believe that knowing as much as I do about Camila enhances my capacity to carry out this analysis, but how confident can I be? I wonder whether I am being sufficiently objective about my findings and conclusions or whether my closeness with Camila prevents me from achieving this. I also wonder about the level of detail with which I ought to describe my relationship with Camila when I write the report. I do not want to misguide or misrepresent the context of my study. Yet I also have a very real interest in publishing the case study I have written. Such a publication would not only help me to obtain tenure but would, I believe, make a significant contribution to the field.

I also have ethical concerns regarding my relationship with Camila. I cannot ignore that my roles as Camila's professor and, later on, mentor and researcher have an impact on our respective status. Given what I know about Latino culture, I must also face the fact that my age and gender certainly reinforce our status differences. Thus, I wonder whether Camila truly had an opportunity to decline to participate in the study, especially given the manner in which I approached her with this idea. I wonder whether as Camila's mentor and friend I should have insisted more vigorously about the potential benefits of her playing a more active role as co-presenter or co-author. Finally, I wonder whether it was ethical for me to begin this study without anyone reviewing it for potential ethical problems. The manner in which the study came about makes it difficult to determine when it began and when it would have been appropriate to undergo such review.

Expectations about each other in the context of our relationship may in fact be the best possible form of informed consent. I am convinced that we have both learned a great deal about and from each other by examining narratives about learning to teach and teaching and ethnicity.[3] Yet I continue to struggle to find an ethically certain position as a researcher and as Camila's teacher, mentor, colleague, and friend.

---

[3] See chapter 10 in Clandinin and Connelly's (2000) *Narrative Inquiry* for an examination of ethical and related concerns in narrative inquiry research that are applicable to inquiry such as the one described in the current case.

CASE five

Commentary on Tomás Galguera's Case

1

Camille Calica
Teacher, Shepherd Elementary School
Hayward, California

Reading this case has been an odd experience because *I am Camila*. Until this point—until having Tomás's perspective on doing this type of work in front of me, in black and white—I was not aware of his struggle. It's clear that though he strives for validity, he also realizes the impact that his personal relationship with me can have on his perspective.

Tomás voices his concern as to whether or not his conclusions will resonate with me. Of course at one level it is impossible for Tomás and me to have the same standards or perspective regarding this study due to the individual roles we play in this specific situation. How is it possible for his account of my experience to be completely valid when he is an outsider looking in? It's not necessarily that Tomás got aspects of the story wrong. But if I were to give my own personal account of my experiences and how those experiences have affected my development as a teacher, my conclusions might look different.

This, in turn, raises a question about the relationship between "getting it right" and the conclusions that can be drawn from Tomás's study about the development of Latina teachers. If I were to challenge his interpretations, I wonder how my input might affect the outcomes of his research, if at all. An issue here is the extent to which, in this type of study, I should be able to highlight what I think is important in my development and to what extent Tomás should or can take my view into account. How would doing so change his conclusions?

What I see is a peculiar dynamic. Tomás hopes to make space between the personal and the impersonal as a means to gain perspective for drawing his conclusions. On the other hand, I hope to make the impersonal more personal so that I can ensure that he "gets it right." In this way, the ethical dilemmas reveal themselves: To what degree should I have the power to set the record straight? If I am given the power, is it possible for Tomás to create a division between his perspective, my personal understanding, and what are determined to be the outcomes of his study?

These dilemmas are present in any research of this nature. What weight does the subject's desire to be correctly understood have in the researcher's interpretation of that subject? It's also true that the subject of any study has his or her own set of assumptions and interpretations, which may also be biased. If input from subjects—what the subjects believe is crucial to know about themselves in relationship to a study—holds great weight and is seriously factored into the final product, what does that say about personal bias? However, if input from the subject is put aside to uphold the agenda of the researcher, is it ethical to publish or make public an outcome that is believed by the subject to be a misinterpretation? These are questions worth thinking about.

2

David M. Donahue
Education
Mills College

I'm grateful to Tomás for telling this story because it captures my own tangled feelings about collaborating with preservice teachers on inquiries into their learning as they enter the profession of teaching. Interestingly, Tomás did not say what his case is "a case of," though his title indicates concerns about validity. When I think about validity in qualitative research, I think less in terms of generalizable knowledge and more in terms of making explicit the process by which that knowledge was gained. Tomás describes his relationship with Camila Calica in terms that strike me as unusual in their candor and that indicate the possible limitations to his findings, giving readers the opportunity to draw their own conclusions about validity.

Reading cases of others' teaching and learning, I find their value comes from the perspective they give me on my own work as much as from the windows they provide on colleagues' thinking. For me, the story Tomás tells is a case of ownership of knowledge and the emotions that arise when we gain personally from someone else's story (in terms of publication credits, tenure, and so on) even while contributing to a fund of knowledge valuable to other researchers and teachers. Perhaps questions about ownership account for the discomfort—maybe even guilt—to which the second part of Tomás's title refers.

Reading this case, I remembered speaking to a group of teacher educators about my work with new teachers and how they learn from their students. Wanting to honor the voices of the new teachers who generously shared their beliefs, opinions, and

> The story Tomás tells is a case of ownership of knowledge and the emotions that arise when we gain personally from someone else's story (in terms of publication credits, tenure, and so on) even while contributing to a fund of knowledge valuable to other researchers and teachers.

experiences with me, my talk was punctuated by many quotes from these teachers. After finishing, I asked for questions and one professor asked, "In telling the stories of your former students, what are you doing to make sure you're not ripping off their stories?" Though not the first time I'd confronted this question, it was the first time I'd been asked in public and I worked hard not to sound defensive. I explained how I gained fully informed consent, how the teachers were free not to participate or to stop participating at any time, how I shared data and my interpretations with the teachers, and how I managed to respect their interpretations when they differed from mine. All the same, the question of ownership lingers with me all of the time in my work on new teachers' learning. As much as this might be a case of validity, it might appropriately be subtitled "Whose Study Is It Anyway?"

I struggle with the difference between relaying teachers' stories and stealing them. Answering the following questions helps me to distinguish between the two.

- Would the teacher have told this story publicly? If the answer is no, then who am I to tell the story?
- What are the benefits to the teacher of making this story public? I am not sure there have to be any. On the other hand, though a publication credit means something very different to a professor seeking tenure than to a public school teacher, I have never met any adults who did not like to see their names in print on something of which they were proud. At a more fundamental level of benefit, did the teacher believe she learned anything by sharing her story?
- What are the drawbacks to the teacher of making this story public? While I might be uncertain about the benefits of telling another teacher's story, I am clear about the drawbacks: There should be none.
- Does the teacher's story address an important question for teacher educators? My main concern is usually about the benefits of the story to the community of teacher educators. If the question or problem really matters, then a story that sheds light deserves public consideration.
- Is the teacher fully aware of what will happen to her story in the research arena? Having one's experience become someone else's text can be as frightening as it is exciting. I remind teachers about their experiences observing and reading about other teachers, how they often brought a critical lens to analyzing those teachers, and how that perspective helped them become more thoughtful, reflective practitioners.
- Does the teacher believe his story is valuable? Because schools isolate teachers from one another, they often say, "This is 'just' my experience." Privileged to work with many teachers and observe their work, I see how their stories represent larger issues in the profession and share that perspective with teachers.
- Do I believe the teacher's story is valuable? Working with teachers, I am re-evaluating the idea of co-

authorship, shifting from a definition of actually writing together to working together to get a story on paper where roles, such as story teller and story writer, are distinct but equal. I wonder if Calica turned down the offer of co-authorship thinking in terms of the former rather than the latter. Perhaps a better model for collaboration can be found in the autobiographies of famous sports figures or movie stars whose books credit them as authors (first author at that!) while also acknowledging that their story is "as told to" another writer. While I don't mean to compare teachers to fleeting celebrities, teachers have even less time than NBA players or Hollywood actors (at least they have an entourage!) to tell their stories.

The feeling of stealing comes not only from putting my name on papers with others' stories but also from lingering guilt about what we as researchers do with those stories—we analyze them. Having taught high school before becoming a teacher educator, I am well aware of a feeling among teachers that analyzing and interpreting teaching is tantamount to criticizing such work. No wonder teachers feel this way when they are so rarely involved in framing research problems or raising the actual questions for research. Rather they are "informants" feeding data to a researcher who has the greater share of control over what happens to their stories. If teachers have more of a say in asking the questions—questions they value and the answers to which they believe would make a difference in their teaching or learning—then their distrust of research would be mitigated. And instead of worrying whether we are ripping off teachers' stories, we might find teachers telling more of their stories, becoming true collaborators in research on their learning and their work, with the commensurate status that comes with contributing to important dialogues in research.

3 Judith Haymore Sandholtz
Education
University of California, Riverside

After reading and pondering this case, I find myself wanting to know more. As is often the situation when analyzing a specific case, I have more questions than answers. This case highlights issues I have encountered in my work but also prompts me to examine dilemmas that I haven't considered. In reflecting on the issues raised by Galguera, I am most intrigued by three main facets of the case.

First, a central aim of Galguera's research is to explore the "learning-to-teach process" for Latino teachers. Culture is clearly an important frame in his study. Early in the case, Galguera writes that the ethics of relationships are culturally dependent. Later, when discussing ethical concerns related to status differences in his relationship with Camila Calica, he focuses primarily on differences in their professional positions and notes that "age and gender enhance my authority over Camila." I wonder to what extent cultural norms influenced perceptions of status in their relationship. What cultural views about authority, age, and gender might be at play here? To what extent does respect for authority vary across cultures? Would age and gender have the same influence if Galguera and Calica did not share the same cultural background, or if that background were not Latino? I also wonder if and how cultural factors contributed to Calica's decision to participate in the study. Galguera questions whether she "truly had an opportunity to decline." Given the cultural framework for the case study itself, I would like to know more about how culture may be influencing status and authority in their relationship.

Second, I am intrigued by underlying assumptions regarding benefits from research. Galguera notes that both he and Calica will learn a substantial amount from participating in the project. However, he states that he will "gain greater recognition and derive more benefits" from publication of the research and worries that he should have pushed harder for Calica to be a co-author or co-presenter. Given the differing institutional demands and rewards for professors and beginning teachers, I wonder what the most significant benefits are for each person in this case. For a professor, research publications are essential for promotion and tenure. For a beginning teacher, effective teaching is of greater consequence. I am reminded of Bob Bullough's 1989 case study of Kerrie Baughman, a first-year teacher who was his former student *(First-Year Teacher: A Case Study)*. The initial study subsequently developed into an extended, collaborative examination of her teach-

ing *("First-Year Teacher" Eight Years Later)*. During a typically tumultuous first year, Baughman discovered that the interviews served as a catalyst to reflect on her teaching. She found that the nonjudgmental questions prompted her to think about aspects of her teaching she hadn't considered and helped her feel more self-assured in her work. In a way, the research became a form of beginning-teacher support that she lacked through a formal program. It was years later, when she was no longer a probationary teacher, that Baughman took on a more collaborative role and co-authorship of publications.

> As an educator, one attempts to guide and influence students in positive ways; but, as a researcher, one aims to be detached and objective. For a former professor of a novice teacher, shifting roles presents particular dilemmas.

For many beginning teachers, the daily pressures and uncertainties of teaching are challenging, if not overwhelming. If participating in research provides a means of alleviating those uncertainties and enhancing professional competence, that may be the most important benefit at the time. The energy and time required to co-author and present research may add another layer of uncertainty and pressure that results in few direct, institutional rewards for a beginning teacher and may potentially pose risks to her success in the classroom. By proposing, but not insisting on, co-authorship, Galguera may have taken the most responsible approach.

Third, I am interested in the potential conflicts in combining roles as educator and researcher when working closely with a beginning teacher. Galguera's initial role was as an educator while Calica was a student in the teacher-education credential program. Though he had not yet decided to do a case study, he was collecting extensive data through the teaching and supervising processes. I wonder at what point he felt his role shift to that of researcher (when the proposal was submitted? when it was accepted?) and how that shift affected both the data he collected and his relationship with Calica. For instance, as a researcher he continued to observe her teaching and to hold debriefing sessions as he did while her student-teacher supervisor. But to what extent did he continue to guide her development and make suggestions regarding her classroom instruction? Did she sense a difference in their interactions?

As an educator, one attempts to guide and influence students in positive ways; but, as a researcher, one aims to be detached and objective. For a former professor of a novice teacher, shifting roles presents particular dilemmas. In conducting the case study I referred to earlier, Bullough decided it was not ethically responsible to withhold information that could prevent serious difficulty for the teacher being observed or her students. Though they both understood that Bullough was not functioning in a teacher role, he responded to Baughman's questions, occasionally passed on important insights, and shared his written interpretations as a source of feedback for her. In his written work, Bullough attempted to be clear about the nature of his influence on the study but acknowledged that he might be criticized as a researcher for that influence. As Galguera points out, such criticism could prevent publication of his case study of Calica. He believes his extensive knowledge of Calica enhances his research, but he admits it may also limit his objectivity. His decisions about how to describe the context of the study have implications for how others review his work.

Given the ethical issues, it may be tempting simply to avoid conducting case studies of former students. But as educators and researchers, our ultimate ethical responsibility is to engage in work that we deem important rather than that which is uncomplicated or sure to succeed.

Resources

Bullough, R. V., Jr. *First-Year Teacher: A Case Study.* New York: Teachers College Press, 1989.

Bullough, R. V., Jr., and Baughman, K. *"First-Year Teacher" Eight Years Later: An Inquiry into Teacher Development.* New York: Teachers College Press, 1997.

Clandinin, D. J., and Connelly, F. M. *Narrative Inquiry: Experience and Story in Qualitative Research.* San Francisco: Jossey-Bass, 2000.

Gordon, June A. *The Color of Teaching.* New York: Routledge Falmer, 2000.

Shulman, Judith H. "Now You See Them, Now You Don't: Anonymity Versus Visibility in Case Studies of Teachers." *Educational Researcher*, 1990, 19(5), 11–15.

Soltis, J. F. "The Ethics of Qualitative Research." In E. W. Eisner and A. Peshkin (eds.), *Qualitative Inquiry in Education: The Continuing Debate.* New York: Teachers College Press, 1990.

Yin, Robert K. *Case Study Research: Design and Methods.* 2nd Ed. Thousand Oaks, Calif.: Sage, 1994.

CASE SIX

From Private to Public Classrooms: "Inadequate" Student Texts in the Scholarship of Teaching and Learning

James E. Seitz
English
University of Pittsburgh

There is a standard narrative in scholarship devoted to pedagogy that goes like this: At the beginning of the semester, students were struggling … then the teacher helped them to see the light … and now, as evidence of how far they progressed, the teacher offers a sample of student writing that displays notable accomplishment, thereby demonstrating the success of the teacher's pedagogy.

I'm sure I am not the first to weary of this narrative. Not only does it oversimplify the relationship between pedagogy and student achievement, but it also tends to efface differences among students in any given course, some of whom may well respond positively to a particular teacher or method at the same time that others remain detached, skeptical, and seemingly unaffected by the same approach the teacher's narrative celebrates. It is these latter, often unmentioned students whom I find myself wondering about whenever I read yet another tale of pedagogical "success": Where are *they* in the seemingly countless stories of classroom triumph? Are we to imagine all student papers in a given class were as impressive (even after revision, at the end of the term) as the one or two exemplary texts the teacher brings forward?

It was with such questions in mind that I decided while writing a book a few years ago on the teaching of English that whatever samples of student work I included would highlight unresolved difficulties in teaching and learning rather than difficulties overcome. I wanted to compose a different kind of pedagogical narrative, one that acknowledged my bewilderment when confronted with college students whose writing seemed stuck in eighth-grade habits of mind and expression—habits that were all the more intractable after

---

James Seitz is associate professor of English at the University of Pittsburgh, where he serves as director of the composition program. In his writing, research, and teaching, he is particularly interested in the intersections among literature, literacy, and liberal education. He is a 2001 Carnegie Scholar.

Respondents

Christie Raney begins graduate studies in education at Ursuline College in summer 2002. She attended the University of Pittsburgh for her undergraduate work in English and has a bachelor of fine arts in theatrical directing from Baylor University.

Mariolina Rizzi Salvatori, a 1999 Carnegie Scholar, is associate professor of English at the University of Pittsburgh, where she teaches undergraduate courses in pedagogy, literacy, hermeneutics, and reception theories.

Annette Seitz is a fellow at the Institute for Learning at the University of Pittsburgh. Her work with the institute focuses primarily on writing instruction (kindergarten through twelfth grade) with a particular emphasis on studying student work to assess student progress, guide instruction, and develop a deeper understanding of standards.

CASE SIX

so many years of practice. I thought it important that representations of courses in composition and literature acknowledge not only those students who make admirable progress as writers during the course of a fifteen-week semester but also those who write the same lifeless, perfunctory prose in December that they wrote in August, and who at times give the impression that pedagogy is beside the point. Indeed, the more I observed these latter students in classes and reread their papers, the more it occurred to me that the problems I was confronting, precisely because they were systemic rather than idiosyncratic, were larger than what any one teacher, no matter how thoughtful or creative, could fully address. The narrative I would write *couldn't* be a narrative in which I posed a "solution," not simply because I didn't have one but because there wasn't one to be had, at least not one that could be achieved by an individual teacher alone.

But if I wanted to do more than allude to the kinds of student writing that posed such a challenge—that is, if I wanted to illustrate the problems I discerned through particular examples—then I would need to quote from student texts that were less than flattering to their writers. Or to put this more bluntly, I would need to display "inadequate" student writing in my book, writing that would be shared not because of its accomplishment but because of its failure. Rather than asking my readers to confirm a pedagogical job well done, I would be asking them to recognize persistent difficulties we often face in the teaching of English.

> If the purpose of citing student texts is to advance academic conversation about teaching and learning, then we cannot say beforehand what forms of citation will serve this purpose, any more than we can say beforehand what form of citation from literary texts will advance academic conversation about literature. Some forms will surely be celebratory, but others will no doubt be critical.

Ultimately, I did go on to publish a book that included samples of student writing that seemed to me to indicate such difficulties. Yet I have continued to wonder, as I did at the time, about two ethical issues that attend this potentially questionable scholarly practice. The first issue concerns the relationship between my portrayal of inept student writing and the endless river of publications over the last two decades that bemoan the state of knowledge and literacy among students at all levels, K through college. When the authors of these publications examine student work, they commonly highlight examples of student ignorance in response to questions on standardized tests: students who don't know in what century the American Civil War occurred or who can't locate Japan on a map or who think that Teddy Roosevelt was a baseball player. When it comes to student writing, the examples are similarly negative: students who don't know "how to write a sentence" or "how to compose an argument" or "how to express themselves clearly." Readers are expected to be appalled by such findings, while at the same time, I believe, to experience smug satisfaction that they themselves have been properly educated.

I knew I was running the risk that my book would be identified with publications of this sort. After all, wasn't I bringing forward samples of student writing in service of a lament? Indeed I was. But it was here that I saw how I could work to distinguish my project from others that are rife with examples of impoverished student knowledge or skills—for while their lament is usually that students today are inferior to students of yesteryear (which thus means we need to return to yesteryear's educational practices), my lament is that the *structure of our curriculum* does not—and never did—do justice to students' latent intelligence (which thus means we need to look forward more than backward as we consider educational reform). Highlighting this difference between my perspective and that of others who are critical of today's students became crucial to how I framed the specific samples of student writing to which I turned in the course of my analysis.

The second ethical issue that I confronted is more complex. Posed as a set of questions, it raises a number of unsettling concerns: Would the students from whose work I quoted have granted me permission to do so had they known how their work would be portrayed? Had I tricked them into consenting to place their weaker—rather than their stronger—writing on public display? Should I explicitly inform students in subsequent courses before they sign permission forms that I have quoted from student writing in order to discuss its inadequacies and not just its accomplishments? Ultimately, to what extent should students be in control of the precise ways their writing is portrayed in their teacher's scholarship? Is it unethical to "borrow" student work for purposes they may not appreciate?

I don't have, nor do I think we can find, secure, final answers to these questions—that is to say, answers suitable to all contexts. But what I can provide are reasons why I resist the notion that we should uniformly quote student work only when we can display that work in a positive light. It seems to me that if the purpose of citing student texts is to advance academic conversation about teaching and learning, then we cannot say beforehand what forms of citation will serve this purpose, any more than we can say beforehand what forms of citation from literary texts will advance academic conversation about literature. Some forms will surely be celebratory, but others will no doubt be critical.

In my book, for instance, I presented two student texts as examples of writing that failed to recognize their use of metaphorical discourse—but I did so to extend discussion of the role of metaphor in the English studies curriculum, not to criticize the student writers themselves. Moreover, I believe these texts were among the best resources available for illustrating the negative consequences of our current curriculum in college English departments, which unwisely separates the presumably metaphorical (literature) from the presumably literal (composition). The blame fell, in other words, not on the students for their inadequate writing but on the curriculum for its inadequate ways of educating students in the dynamics of literacy.

None of this is meant to dismiss concern over the ethical issues raised by scholarship that quotes from student work. However I may defend my use of student writing for purposes of reforming a troubled curriculum, it remains a practice about which we must continue to reflect. I'd like to conclude by suggesting that part of the difficulty we face when considering the ethics of quotation lies in the ambiguous status of the texts produced (by teacher as well as student) in a college course. Should these texts be considered part of the public domain, to be treated as we treat academic sources in the library? Or should they be considered

private documents, "owned" by individuals who may prevent them from being accessed by others? In what ways are syllabi, assignments, exams, student papers, class discussions, and so on, commodities that belong to individual teachers and students, and in what ways are they public resources available to all for perusal and evaluation? We have a tendency to think of the classroom as a closed space, a place where the teachers can shut the door and create a private domain with their students. But the scholarship of teaching and learning, which requires scrutiny of both pedagogical materials and student work, would appear to challenge this view of the classroom.

As a teacher of composition, I have long been accustomed to quoting from student writing in my scholarship and to requesting that students sign forms that grant me permission to do so. Indeed, distributing permission forms has become almost as routine as distributing a syllabus—something I do every semester, for virtually every course I teach. Yet that hasn't made it any easier to answer the questions that accompany this practice, particularly those regarding the limits I might place on my use of student work. My aim to expand the range of pedagogical narratives found in the scholarship of teaching and learning may be worth pursuing—but the place of student writing within those narratives remains difficult to determine.

james
SEITZ

Commentary on James Seitz's Case

1. Christie Raney
Student, English and Education
University of Pittsburgh

As a current university student and future teacher, my perspective on the ethical issues in the scholarship of teaching and learning is of a dual nature.

My first response to Dr. Seitz's case is from a student point of view: Could I (or any student) be harmed by the publication of a "less than flattering" example of my writing? It seems highly unlikely that a student would ever be affected by, or even know about, such use of his or her work; however, this fanciful pondering of possibilities leads me to a series of more procedural questions that are not touched on in this case. How much information is given to the student before he or she signs a permission form? What does the permission form say? How is anonymity guaranteed? Do safeguards exist to protect against the misuse of student writing samples? While I do not believe it is necessary to explicitly state in the permission form that "poor" writing samples will be used, certainly a thorough explanation of the project would imply this possibility. As long as adequate information is given to the student prior to signing a permission form, and as long as anonymity is strictly maintained, then using examples of poor student writing is an acceptable practice.

My perspective as a future teacher is slightly different, but it reaches the same conclusion. That is, while I am concerned about protecting students' privacy, and respecting their work, I also worry about one-sided, thus inaccurate, scholarship on the teaching of writing. If only the celebratory use of writing examples is considered ethical, then no examples at all should be used. As a future teacher seeking guidance from those with more experience, I want to know the whole story—the successes and the failures. The question of how to deal with the failures is vital to the ongoing story of how to create the successes. If scholarship is to be of any help in the field of teaching and learning, it will need to be clear, unbiased, balanced, and accurate. It must tell the whole story.

2. Mariolina Rizzi Salvatori
English
University of Pittsburgh

In the name of the ethics of the profession—in the name, that is, of recording practices that can give a more accurate sense of what the work of teaching entails and what makes it possible—Jim Seitz calls for theoretical accounts of teaching that do not exclusively focus on a teacher's success and on students' accomplishments as markers of that success. The function of these alternative accounts would be to make visible that which our stories of success leave out, that is, records of student writing that, although they cannot be read as examples of accomplishment, can and should be studied to advance understanding for teacher and student alike. Writing these accounts, however, raises for teachers a set of intricate problems that Seitz names the "ethics of quotation" in representations of student work. What Seitz's case dramatizes is that a teacher's ethical practice of asking for students' consent to cite from their work is not sufficient in and of itself, since students often sign their consent not fully knowing that their writing could be used in ways they might find embarrassing. What position should we take on this matter? Is a student's potential embarrassment to be ignored in the interest of advancing the scholarship of teaching and learning? Seitz's conclusion invites serious consideration: "My aim to expand the range of pedagogical narratives found in the scholarship of teaching and learning may be worth pursuing—but the place of student writing within those narratives remains difficult to determine."

Reading Seitz's case, I have been thinking about a particular aspect of the ethics of the profession.

I have been thinking about the "teaching function" that these accounts of classroom practice are often assigned. I have been thinking, specifically, about the large number of new teachers who every year are assigned to teach without appropriate preparation, and who often read this literature for help, but without any guidance, and nobody to share their doubts and anxieties with. And I have been reminded of how many times new teachers have told me that stories of success can make them feel even more inadequate. I am not trying to undermine teachers' narratives of success: They can be valuable, they can be inspirational, and they can help correct common figurations of teachers as cynical, sadistic, bureaucratic, dim-witted, and insufficiently literate. But,

> In the name of the ethics of the profession, I am arguing for experienced teachers to make visible to others the intrinsic difficulties of teaching. But for these difficulties not to be perceived and internalized as failures...a different understanding of difficulties will be needed.

especially in light of the teaching function that success narratives fulfill, absent appropriate programs of teacher preparation, I share Seitz's desire to balance them with accounts of teaching that focus on and explore, more realistically, both students' writing and teachers' plans that go awry.

Am I arguing then for stories of failure? Of course not. In the name of the ethics of the profession, I am arguing instead for experienced teachers to make visible to others the intrinsic difficulties of teaching. But for these difficulties not to be perceived and internalized as failures—by the rest of the profession, by the culture at large, and particularly by the students whose writing may be included in these accounts—a different understanding of difficulties will be needed.

We need more accounts of teaching that place the learner and learning at center stage. If and when the prior knowledge that students bring to their learning is constructed as indispensable for and integral to their (and their teachers') *further* learning, then we begin to understand teaching not as dispensation but as collaborative formation and transaction of knowledge. That is, we begin to see and to practice teaching as a process that is never completely predictable because it depends on the interaction of three agencies of equal import and value—the teacher, the student, and the knowledge they together produce as they study and discuss ideas and issues generated by a course's subject matter. In this complex interaction, many things can happen that were not planned, and many things may not happen as they had been scheduled, but some of these things can turn out to be opportunities to understand learning, and teaching, differently.

Is what I am proposing difficult? Yes. But to assume or to pretend that teaching is *not* difficult is both inaccurate and counterproductive. That it is inaccurate becomes evident as soon as we allow ourselves to leave behind anachronistic models of teaching (as didactic, hierarchical, based on the assumption that the teacher is the one who knows, the student the one who does not know, that knowledge is measurable and transmittable, that intelligence is quantifiable, that learning is a function of attitude, and will power, personality, I.Q., etc.). And the assumption is counterproductive because it ignores the potential of acknowledging and understanding the function of difficulty in the learning process. It associates difficulty with lack of knowledge and faulty learning—characteristics usually attributed to mediocre students—and in so doing it promotes a warped understanding of how humans learn, what makes learning possible, significant, and enduring.

Seitz's concern with the ethics of citation (of student texts) deserves our attention. Accurate, responsible citation is a fundamental aspect of traditional scholarship. It must be a fundamental aspect of the scholarship of teaching, even as (in fact particularly when) the ethics of citation raise the ethical difficulties that Seitz's research and writing bring forth. I hope we don't call these difficulties "intractable" and put them aside. One way of engaging and responding to Seitz's provocation is by learning to teach ourselves and our students to frame difficulties as inevitable and productive phases of learning, at every stage of learning. A professional culture that understands difficulty in these terms would greatly alleviate the tension Seitz so poignantly identifies, not by sidestepping difficulty as an ethical issue, but by demonstrating what's to be gained—individually, professionally, programmatically, institutionally, culturally, and emotionally—when investigating it in such different terms.

3. Annette Seitz
Resident Fellow, Institute for Learning
Learning Research and Development Center
University of Pittsburgh

For the past six years, I have been working with school districts around the country on reforming their curricula through professional development sessions that often make use of student work. This experience has led me to believe that if we are to "go public" with teaching and learning, then we must share our students' work not just to celebrate what is working in instruction but also to figure out how we can do a better job. Within a community of practice, there are multiple reasons for studying samples of student work. For example, a faculty may study work to identify what "successful" means within their community (e.g., writing in a math course that shows successful problem solving; writing in a literature course that demonstrates a student's deep understanding of the text), to learn about content, or to articulate expectations. They may meet and discuss their own student samples in order to practice assessing what a group of students' learning needs are and brainstorm together what would help these students become more proficient. That is, as a community they might design curriculum and instruction specifically to meet these students' needs. In fact, in an ideal situation, teachers periodically study their own student work samples and plan instruction together, then reflect afterwards (again using student work samples) on the effectiveness of that instruction, and plan for future instruction.

Inherent in this list of activities is a developmental continuum: Teachers move from models of successful student performance to more and more problematic examples. Using this type of model-to-problems framework also allows for the teaching community to develop its own norms for discussing student work in a respectful way. In many communities I have worked with, the norm is for the samples to have all names and identifying indicators removed before they are brought to the group. This is important for developing a risk-free environment where teachers can feel safe about sharing their own students' work while the norms for discussing work are being established. This also gives students protection through anonymity.

But I would like to suggest that our worries about sharing work that we consider problematic come from our persistent belief that the student's work is a reflection of the student alone and not her teacher, her teacher last year, all her teachers back to Ms. O'Boyce in kindergarten, the curriculum she has access to, the whole school system she is in and the way that system perceives her because of her gender, race, economic background, her family, and so on. The quality of the work has little to do with us—unless it is good.

While I find the medical analogy attractive—that like a team of doctors we mull over a student's work, assess strengths and shortcomings, and diagnose next instructional steps—a medical analogy is limited in that it implies the patient's passivity. And that is not what I want to suggest in regard to students. Let's imagine an ideal situation where members of a faculty or community of practice believe that they are all (though not equally) responsible for the learning of their students, their colleagues in the community, and also for the learning of the students in their colleagues' classrooms. From this perspective, a student text is not simply about a particular student's limitations but is a diagnostic to inform a team of teachers about what she already knows and what course of action (with the student's informed and active engagement in the process) would support her continued development as a writer, reader, mathematician, etc. This learning is not only of value to the student and her teacher, it becomes a concrete, shared problem and solution for the community and a shorthand reference for the learning surrounding the piece (e.g., teachers may refer to subsequent similar problems by the name of a piece of student work).

If we mean to establish effective professional communities, then we must facilitate conversations that

quickly move from "this is the ideal" to "here is a problem; how can we solve it?" I would like to argue that it is the work a group does around samples that are not perfect that fosters rigorous, self-reflective conversations that promote teachers' learning generally and the active use of student work for lesson planning in particular. The sooner the problems that the group has to solve are aligned with their own students' needs, their curriculum, etc., the more effective and sustainable professional development will become. Studying samples that are problematic gives all of us practice with the real work of teaching, analyzing student learning through their written work to reflect on and design instruction. Working on samples that are "on the way" also adds to teachers' commitment to the process because these samples look more like the work of "*real* students." For professional communities to stand a chance of being effective in improving classroom practice, the samples must embody many of the specific problems teachers experience with their own students.

Central to all discussions about student work is the question, what do we want to learn? If the purpose is to learn about content, then studying samples both successful and unsuccessful is crucial to reaching consensus on what the community means by "successful" in a particular content area at this particular level. But if we are studying student work to reflect and learn more about instruction, then it is disrespectful to study work without the assignment, circumstances of performance, information on the specific prior instruction, where the class is in the larger arc of instruction, and what the teacher's purpose (anticipated student learning) is for this assignment. Taking a piece out of context to reflect on instruction pushes us back into thinking that the student is totally responsible for his or her work.

But what if our ethical agonizing was really about stance? What if using samples that are problematic were sincerely about our own learning to be better teachers? What if the members of the community we shared these samples with saw themselves as accountable to help us solve a general problem about pedagogy and not how to "cure" the student? The short answer might be: Could we have this conversation with the student who produced the work in the room?

As members of this extended community of practice, we have an obligation continually to reflect on our practice by studying what and how our students are learning. And what they are not. And as we begin the twenty-first century, we have an increasing number of exciting venues for sharing our work and our problems, including internet Web sites, video, and CD-ROMs to name a few. We *must* give up the idea that we can do all of this alone without communal discussion of both successful and unsuccessful student work.

Resources

Blythe, T.; Allen, D.; and Powell, B. S. *Looking Together at Student Work: A Companion Guide to Assessing Student Learning.* New York: Teachers College Press, 1999.

Clare, Lindsey, and Aschbacher, Pamela R. "Exploring the Technical Quality of Using Assignments and Student Work as Indicators of Classroom Practice." *Educational Assessment,* 2001, 7(1), 39–59. Send requests for reprints to Lindsey Clare, CRESST/UCLA Center for the Study of Evaluation, 301 GSE&IS, Box 9515222, Los Angeles, CA 90095.

Elam, Helen Reguerio. "The Difficulty of Reading." In Alan C. Purves (ed.), *The Idea of Difficulty in Literature.* New York: SUNY, 1991.

Gadamer, Hans-Georg. *Philosophical Hermeneutics.* (David E. Linge, trans. and ed.) Berkeley: University of California Press, 1976.

Newkirk, Thomas. "Looking for Trouble: A Way to Unmask Our Readings." *College English,* 1984, 46, 756–766.

Salvatori, Mariolina Rizzi. "Towards a Hermeneutics of Difficulty." In Louise Z. Smith (ed.), *Audits of Meaning.* Portsmouth, N.H.: Boynton/Cook, 1988.

———. "Understanding Difficulty: A Heuristic." In Jeffrey R. Galin, Carol Peterson Haviland, and J. Paul Johnson (eds.), *Teaching/Writing in the Late Age of Print.* Boston: Hampton, 2002.

Seitz, James E. *Motives for Metaphor: Literacy, Curriculum Reform, and the Teaching of English.* Pittsburgh: University of Pittsburgh Press, 1999.

———. "From Dismay to Collaboration: Reimagining the Student in Higher Education." *ADE Bulletin*, 2001, Winter(127): 41–43.

Steiner, George. *On Difficulty and Other Essays.* New York: Oxford University Press, 1978.

Internet Resources

Coalition of Essential Schools/Looking Collaboratively at Student Work: An Essential Toolkit. [http://www.essentialschools.org/pubs/horace/13/v13n02.html]. November 1996.

"Looking at Student Work: A Project of the Annenberg Institute for School Reform." [http://www.lasw.org/protocols.html]. N.d.

CASE SEVEN

Going Public with Students' Work: The Movie

Sherry Linkon
English and American Studies
Youngstown State University

I am currently engaged in a multiyear, multiple-iteration research project aimed at developing strategies and tools for enhancing student learning in interdisciplinary courses. As part of this effort, I have gathered a variety of data—surveys, student work, interviews, videotapes of students working in groups—from several classes in American Studies and English. At the beginning of each course, I have explained my research project to students in general ways and then distributed a written description and a consent form. Both on the form and in my explanation of my research, I note that I may use excerpts from students' work, including clips of the videos, in online and print publications. I emphasize that students may choose not to complete the surveys, participate in interviews, or have their work included or cited in the study with no penalty, and I promise to make any public references to their work anonymous. I also explain that the purpose of my research is both to enhance my own teaching and to help other teachers, and I make clear that I will write and talk about students' experiences to an audience of other faculty who teach interdisciplinary courses, and that the focus of my presentation of their work will not be on evaluating them but helping faculty learn how to teach better.

One component of my work—as part of a larger national project—is to develop, assess, and interrogate the uses of technology in teaching courses on history and culture. The national project has used grant funding to hire a filmmaker (John Stern, who is one of the respondents to this case) to produce a documentary that will

---

Sherry Linkon is a 1999 Carnegie Scholar and Youngstown State University campus coordinator for the Visible Knowledge Project, a national research project investigating teaching and learning with technology in humanities courses. Her research focuses on working-class pedagogy, representations of class and work in the United States, and critical explorations of student learning in interdisciplinary courses.

Respondents

Randy Bass is associate professor of English and executive director of the Center for New Designs in Learning and Scholarship at Georgetown University. He also directs the Visible Knowledge Project, a national scholarship of teaching initiative exploring the impact of new technologies on learning in the humanities. He has been working with new media pedagogies and faculty development since the late 1980s and was selected as a Carnegie Scholar in 1998.

Thomas Hatch is a senior scholar at the Carnegie Foundation where he co-directs the K–12 Carnegie Academy for the Scholarship of Teaching and Learning and leads the work of the Carnegie Knowledge Media Lab. His current research focuses on K–12 school reform and on new strategies for documenting and exchanging the intellectual work of teaching and learning, especially through multimedia.

John Stern is president of West Peak Media, where he focuses on education research, training, and policy videotapes. He has produced a variety of programs exploring innovative K–12 teaching and university research on the effects of teaching on learning.

CASE seven

include case studies of faculty research and student learning related to the uses of technology in history and culture courses. My work will be one of those case studies. The filmmaker interviewed me, some colleagues, and a few of my students, and he filmed a class session in which students worked with online resources. Students were given the option of not being filmed, and all of those who were filmed signed release forms from the filmmaker that granted permission for the film to be used by the grant-funded project. At the start of the class session being taped, we asked for volunteers to be the focal point of the film. Two young men—good friends and fraternity brothers—volunteered.

During the session, students worked through a set of prompts to examine a digital map with technical tools to allow viewers to zoom in on specific details. The map—from the nineteenth century—served as an introduction to local history, and the prompts invited students to make guesses based on what they saw in the map and their prior knowledge of the community. We hadn't, up to this point, worked with maps before, nor had we talked much yet about local history. The activity was not designed to assess their knowledge or even to teach specific information but rather to open our class inquiry into local history. Although the two students who were filmed struggled to move beyond identifying familiar places on the map, which is where nearly all of the class began, they also later speculated about what the map showed about the history of race, ethnicity, religion, and work in the local community, which is exactly what I had hoped would happen. Their speculations revealed some misinformation or—perhaps a more accurate way of putting it—showed how much their understanding of the past was shaped and in some ways limited by their knowledge of the present and their experiences with family and local culture. In addition, perhaps because they were aware of the camera or perhaps because they successfully ignored it, and because they were friends, their interactions were very casual and rather funny. They argued freely, they used slang, and they talked fairly comfortably about history, clearly unaware that some of what they said was incomplete or inaccurate.

From my perspective as a researcher, the video was very useful. It clarified some issues about how students used the map and the technology through which the map was made available, and it highlighted some issues related to prior knowledge and the value of teaching about local culture. In part because it showed two students struggling with the assignment, it also helped me consider the question of how to balance directed instruction with independent inquiry.

A few months later, at a summer institute for participants in the national project, the project director, Randy Bass, whose response follows, and I developed a workshop on framing research questions and making sense of various kinds of evidence of student learning. We used several clips from the classroom video as examples. I made careful selections from the ninety-minute video to highlight a couple of key points related to how the two students moved from simply "getting their bearings" with the map to beginning to speculate about who lived in the local community in 1880, what life was like here at that time, and how their prior knowledge shaped their speculations. In the workshop, however, I did not provide much introduction to the clips, because the purpose of the workshop was for participants to generate questions and interpretations based on what they saw, not to hear my interpretations. I wanted to show how one piece of evidence can open up many possible inquiries, but I also wanted to emphasize how difficult it is to draw valid conclusions

based on one piece of evidence. I felt that the best way to do that was to show the video clips and invite discussion without providing a lot of my own interpretation or evaluation in advance. The workshop went well, and the clips worked very much as I had hoped. Participants raised a number of researchable questions based on what they saw, and they offered a variety of interpretations. This led into a useful discussion about different kinds of evidence, the value of triangulation, and the idea that scholarship of teaching and learning isn't necessarily about whether a specific assignment was effective but rather about understanding how students learn.

But I was surprised and distressed by one aspect of my colleagues' response to the video. Much of what these two students said generated laughter—in part, I think, because of their style of interaction but also because of their fumbling and errors. I'll admit that I laughed along with others—laughter can be infectious that way, and, as I said, the interactions *were* funny—but the more I thought about what happened, the more uncomfortable I felt. I'm sure that when the students signed the release forms and when they entrusted me with their work, they didn't expect that a roomful of academics would be laughing at them. One of the guiding principles, I think, of using students' work is that we should treat it and them with respect, and our responses to the video clips were not very respectful.

> I'm nervous about seeming to present these two students as fools. I want to treat these students with respect and to encourage my colleagues to do so, yet it's also true that showing the students' errors is part of the point here.

Now the project wants to put these video clips on the Web, as part of an online version of the workshop. As in the workshop, I don't want to provide an extensive introduction to the clips because I don't want to limit the kinds of questions and inquiry the video might prompt. I suspect that individuals watching the online version will be less likely to laugh than those at the workshop, since people tend to laugh more in a group than when they are alone, but I'm nervous about seeming to present these two students as fools. I want to treat these students with respect and to encourage my colleagues to do so, yet it's also true that showing the students' errors is part of the point here. I think the clips will be a valuable resource for my colleagues, but I also wonder if I need to provide some commentary about how we respond to them. Is it enough and is it even appropriate to say something overt about this on the Web site? If so, what do I say?

CASE seven

Commentary on Sherry Linkon's Case

1

Randy Bass
English and American Studies
Georgetown University

As the director of the national grant-funded project mentioned in Sherry Linkon's case, I have reflected a lot about the "laughter incident" at the summer institute she describes. From my perspective, several things are at stake in this episode. First and foremost are the ethical dimensions of using student work (especially videotape evidence) as part of the process of inquiry into teaching and learning. Obviously, anonymity is difficult with visual evidence; yet such evidence is effective in classroom research precisely because it is vivid, immediate, and almost intimate. Problems arise when that intimacy becomes the focus of public scholarly exchange in a faculty development context. As a project director who is trying to engage large numbers of faculty in the scholarship of teaching and learning, I am both sensitive to the ethical questions and anxious about anything that might inhibit or complicate work that already faces great resistance as a mainstream practice. If we can't share evidence, especially evidence revelatory of partial student understanding, then we cannot build a serious, communal discourse about learning. Thus, the issues raised by Sherry's case have serious implications for the heart of this enterprise.

Let me offer a slightly strange analogy. When giving presentations on teaching and learning I often show a clip from the movie *Ferris Bueller's Day Off*, that classic 1980s expression of suburban scholastic ennui. The scene I show depicts a high school social-science teacher, played brilliantly by the deadpan Ben Stein, lecturing cluelessly to a roomful of students with blank or hostile expressions. Throughout the scene, Stein prattles on, asking rhetorical questions, oblivious to the fact that the students are utterly disengaged. Each time I show this film clip it evokes lots of laughter. It is a caricature of mind-numbing education, evoking a kind of primal scene of teaching—the worst-case scenario we all fear or dread, the baseline above which we all assume we perform. I showed this clip recently as an ice breaker for a faculty workshop on active learning. When the clip ended, one of the professors said self-deprecatingly and almost confessionally: "Been there."

I mention this in the context of Sherry's case because I think there is a connection between the laughter evoked by the clip from *Ferris Bueller* and the laughter in the workshop session where Sherry's classroom clips were shown. Obviously the contexts of the clips are quite different, and the laughter evoked by Sherry's classroom scenes of a different order. The *Ferris Bueller* clip is supposed to be funny, and my intention in showing it is to get the audience to laugh—both at Ben Stein and a little at themselves. And that gets us here to the point. In the case of the summer institute, and the project participants watching Sherry's student clips, I don't believe that the laughter had anything to do with condescension, arrogance, or ridicule. (I think the students' own joking style had a lot to do with licensing the audience's laughter.) No, I can't speak for everyone, but my sense was that this laughter was more about the energy release of a roomful of smart, dedicated teachers who care a lot about student learning, and who—when bearing witness to two earnest and slightly hammy students—made an unwitting collective declaration that they had all "been there."

More importantly, I believe that the institute audience's laughter is inseparable from the anxiety produced in faculty when they begin to engage in the scholarship of teaching and learning. That is, I think their laughter was as much about themselves as the students they were watching. Video evidence of student learning evokes emotions about the exposure of one's own practice. Sherry's questions are not just questions about the use and framing of student work; they point us to the many layers of exposure, vulnerability, and performance at stake in doing the scholarship of teaching and learning.

That being said, we must operate with certain benchmarks about how we present student work. I have used the clips of Sherry's class a few times in my own public presentations and workshops. In the wake of the summer institute, I have been cautious not only to frame the clips thoroughly but to inoculate against runaway laughter. I explain exactly what is in the clips, how a couple of the students are a little lost and perhaps performing somewhat for the camera. But then I also explain what kind of learn-

> Anonymity is difficult with visual evidence; yet such evidence is effective in classroom research precisely because it is vivid, immediate, and almost intimate. Problems arise when that intimacy becomes the focus of public scholarly exchange in a faculty development context.

ing I see in the clips. Most importantly I make a strong pitch for the value of seeing these selections, but caution against making any judgments about so narrow a moment in so complex a process. I also remind people of how any one of us might be uncomfortable having others judge our students' learning by seeing only a snippet of it out of context.

Learning how to properly frame and contextualize will take time and experience. Last fall, I showed a videotape of my students engaged in think-aloud exercises, as part of a retreat for Georgetown faculty. One particular clip showed two students struggling to make sense of a difficult historical text. I had a very specific, well-thought-out context for showing it; but the faculty in the audience had only the thinnest context for receiving it. I did not properly frame the clip along the lines I now use for Sherry's materials. And although some faculty in the Georgetown audience found it valuable (even powerful for some), in retrospect, it was a mistake. That audience was not ready to see those clips in the way I had intended.

The lesson is clear: If qualitative (video) evidence of student learning is valuable because it reveals something about a very layered and complicated context, then its use *out of context* has to be treated with more sensitivity than other kinds of evidence. We need to consider carefully the readiness of any given audience to make sense of qualitative evidence of student learning. Given that, we probably also have to make strategic choices about "publication" contexts (a Web-based portfolio for example) where we cannot control the audience. We may have to hold back certain kinds of excellent evidence in publication, even though it might work well live, because its reception cannot properly be qualified.

In addition to developing a rhetoric for framing examples of student work, we need to utilize the technologies that support them (such as streaming video and visual or digital signatures). And beyond these, the more we can associate and integrate the faculty member's meta-commentary with the evidence itself, the less likely bits of evidence are to be taken out of context. But, finally, we have to remember what kind of work this is. I don't think we can go about the scholarship of teaching and learning as if it were a scientific experiment. It is messy and imprecise work about utterly human situations, where the personal and the professional, subjective and objective, are finely meshed. While we need to do everything possible not to betray the trust of our students who are an integral part of this work, we must also remember that the whole enterprise is a work in progress, where we must be prepared to confront our own partial understandings or we will make no progress at all.

2. Thomas Hatch
Senior Scholar
The Carnegie Foundation for
the Advancement of Teaching

Video of classroom interactions, as described by Sherry Linkon, can be a powerful way to represent teaching and learning. Part of the power comes from the fact that we get a sense of the classroom context, a glimpse of the participants, a feel for the activity. Viewers can see and hear things that are hard

CASE seven

to convey in a written report. We can look at the interactions over and over again, examining them from different angles, looking for things we might not have noticed the first time around. Like the "zoomable" digital map that Sherry's students inspect, video allows viewers a little more opportunity to examine and shape what they see in the selections provided for them.

At the same time, these features of video contribute to ethical dilemmas like the one Sherry describes. Videotapes can conjure up emotions—tears and anger as well as laughter—and lead to interpretations

> It is naïve to think that schools and classrooms can or should be completely public spaces. But I have seen too many efforts to improve classroom instruction fail because only the successful elements of the work were documented and displayed. Instead of protecting participants, such efforts to control what others see create suspicions, fears, and tensions that make subsequent discussion difficult, if not impossible.

and conclusions that investigators like Sherry may not be able to anticipate. Furthermore, as John Stern points out in his commentary, because research participants can never be as anonymous in video as they can be in other forms of recording and reporting, the possibility that video participants and their activities may be seen in negative or unflattering ways has to be taken into account.

But, at its root, the dilemma Sherry describes is not unique to video (though solutions like blurring the faces and masking the voices of participants may be). For me, the problem is not simply whether these students can be identified and recognized, or whether or not their actions seem amusing. The question is whether the clips provide a fair representation of their activity. Similarly, while the role of video and other media in blurring the line between private and public spaces is an important issue, the larger question is the extent to which we consider the classroom itself to be a public space.

In addressing these issues, I am of two minds. On the one hand, as a teacher and researcher who has documented and displayed the work of students from preschool through graduate school, I am particularly concerned about negative consequences that could result from any representations of student work; although I want others to be able to view student work and draw their own conclusions, I also don't want the students' behavior or activities to be misconstrued or misunderstood. As a result, in my own work, particularly in work with young students, I have often chosen not to use video, and, in many cases, I have simply decided not to show work or provide descriptions that could cast students in a negative light. I have tried carefully to control what is public and what is not.

At the same time, in my work supporting efforts to improve classroom practice in both K–12 and higher education, I also believe in the fundamental value of making teaching and learning public. I have seen numerous instances where researchers have carefully and effectively depicted the struggles and successes of students and teachers. Usually, they do so with great trepidation, concerned about how those represented will respond. In most cases I know of, researchers have been relieved and surprised to find that the subjects appreciated seeing their activities, good and bad, represented fairly. In one instance, for example, participants in a study of high-school reform felt that their concerns and frustrations were validated by cases that showed how much they were struggling; they wanted others to better understand what they were going through and the difficulties they had to face.

In another instance, Heidi Lyne, a middle school teacher participating in Carnegie's program on the scholarship of teaching and learning, has produced a documentary that depicts the development of a new approach to assessment in which students present a portfolio of their work in an end-of-the-year exhibition. If she did not show the trials, tribulations, and frustrations of the process for both herself and her students, she could not provide a fair representation or help viewers anticipate what they might encounter should they choose to develop a similar system in their own schools and classrooms. As a result, there are times in the documentary where the students' comments (and efforts to evade the work) are amusing, and times when viewers see Heidi pushing and prodding the students more than she would have liked. But the result is that we get a good sense of what the process looks like and what it feels like, as well.

Heidi has controlled, to a certain extent, what and how much of the development of the exhibition process she makes public. But, like Sherry, she also invites viewers to draw conclusions of their own. As a result, neither she, nor Sherry, can control the interpretations and reactions of those who view the clips. But, through their use of video, Heidi and Sherry have created a powerful means of engaging the audience. When even what appear to be fair, responsible depictions create unanticipated and perhaps problematic responses, then opportunities for discussion and analysis arise. These are exactly the kinds of discussions that we need to have in order to build a wider understanding of what goes on in the classroom and what meaningful learning and powerful teaching look like.

It is naive to think that schools and classrooms can or should be completely public spaces. But I have seen too many efforts to improve classroom instruction fail because only the successful elements of the work were documented and displayed. Instead of protecting participants, such efforts to control what others see create suspicions, fears, and tensions that make subsequent discussion difficult, if not impossible. As a result, colleagues, administrators, parents, community members, and even students are cheated of a chance to learn about the innovations and to develop the kind of knowledge that can inform their further development.

Rather than construing classrooms as private spaces to which we occasionally provide access, we might usefully consider the implications of viewing classrooms first and foremost as public spaces. In that context, all of those involved in classroom research need to know that their activities may be public; and those participating in the research as well as those conducting it also need to have the means to restrict public access if necessary. Then we need to provide the context, offer the questions and perspectives, and have the discussions that will enable those who observe what goes on in classrooms to understand what they see.

3 John Stern
Videographer and President
West Peak Media, Inc.

Sherry Linkon and Pat Hutchings asked me to respond to Sherry's case involving faculty reactions to videotape clips produced in her classroom. I had initially taped some of Sherry's students for a videotape commissioned by the Visible Knowledge Project (VKP) at Georgetown University, an effort to engage humanities faculty in scholarly examinations of the effects of technology-enhanced teaching and learning. I attended the workshop Sherry describes and was, as she was, baffled by faculty members who laughed in response to students depicted in the video clips. The concerns Sherry raises about the unexpected faculty response are related to issues that I struggle with as a classroom videographer.

I have taped students and teachers in classrooms for over six years. It is my hope that the classroom videos I produce, whether short clips or longer narrative pieces, help faculty develop thoughtful improvements in teaching practices—and Sherry confirmed that this was true for her. But, in pursuing this aim, I am always concerned about protecting the dignity of those I work with. Like Sherry, I wondered whether the faculty response to students in the clip represented a chuckle of recognition at typical student behavior, or a form of condescension. If the latter, we must ask why and whether the tapes should continue to be shared in more public ways.

The ethical dilemma raised here is the extent to which classroom video belongs in highly public venues like Web sites. To an extent, Sherry dealt with this dilemma by checking the signed consent form we distributed for that purpose and then reaffirming consent with her students. But the issue of how public such video should be reaches beyond signed consent forms, to concerns about the influence of media and new technology on privacy. For instance, production of broadcast entertainment programs

CASE seven

based on documentary techniques is accelerating. Television programs like *Cops* attract viable audiences and are relatively cheap to produce. Surveillance Web sites invite viewers to peer into the daily lives of strangers. These media genres intentionally blur the line between what is public and what is private, and they may have implications for the way researchers think about developing audiences for their work. My own feeling is that researchers contemplating similar broadcast practices need to be very clear about their allied obligations to research participants.

On the other hand, and in spite of these reservations, there are good reasons to make substantive information about student learning at universities and colleges more public than it currently is. Family decisions about college choice are now dominated by institutional marketing and rankings that yield little information about the quality of teaching and learning. More substantive, objective information about efforts to improve student learning may help students and parents select colleges best suited to their

> It seemed to me that hearing how experts recover from errors would be constructive information for novice learners and consistent with the project mission. This was, I suppose, a plea for consistency in the way student and faculty video sequences would be handled.

goals. We need to expand the public literature and public literacy about higher education. And video may be a powerful medium for achieving this goal.

Which brings me to the topic of why (in light of difficulties already noted above) faculty members like Sherry might go to the trouble of using a camera to collect data about learning. One reason is that unlike low-tech research tools, video has the advantage of forthrightly revealing faces and voices, as well as creating relatively accurate records of events. Video can also enrich the research record by making visible certain nuances of the environment that might otherwise go unnoticed. (Imagine what would be lost if the video were simply transcribed: In an attempt to write out nonverbal elements of the scene, Sherry might have added interpretations that others might not see or agree with; vocal intonations in the video, missing from the written text, might alter important meanings.) A further justification for using audio or video is that both are now as portable as text. As a result, video is becoming more useful in professional development workshops like Sherry's, where participants examine primary documents, incidents, or examples played from CD or DVD in order to focus attention on teaching and learning.

But Sherry's case points out the caution that must be employed in such settings. The faculty laughter provoked by the earnest efforts of her students in the video clips really puzzled me. In the video, students use their own informal vernacular and alternate between confidence and ready admission of their own shortcomings as learners. Sherry and her colleague later told me they too were puzzled by the laughter, and a bit irritated with their peers.

Within days of Sherry's screening of the student videotape, I was asked to review video clips of an accomplished faculty member analyzing a document. According to two colleagues from the same field, this faculty member erred in his interpretation. Those watching the video clip wondered if it was fair to make a Web clip from a sequence depicting him in an interpretive error. I suggested going back to the faculty member so that he could provide some comment about his own missteps as a way of helping students understand the role of false starts in scholarship. It seemed to me that hearing how experts recover from errors would be constructive information for novice learners and consistent with the project mission. This was, I suppose, a plea for consistency in the way student and faculty video sequences would be handled.

These incidents seem to illustrate a power differential that exists between undergraduate students and faculty. The ethical problem revolves around the manner in which any videotaped participant should expect to be treated in an investigation of teaching and learning. In discussing their aims with students, scholars of teaching and learning need to be clear about the fact that polished and flattering learning performances are often not the most useful grist for authentic research. Hesitancy, confusion, mistakes, and unrehearsed breakthroughs can be more meaningful as windows into the complex process of teaching and learning. Students (and other participants in the work) need to know that errors will be included and valued by the investigator if they help advance the field and contribute to more effective teaching.

I know that most of those who attended Sherry's VKP seminar traveled great distances to be there. Some found the video clips a cause for laughter, but, after the laughter died down and discussion began, it was clear that viewers really did focus on the substance of the scenes—that is, the tactics used by novice learners to develop historical and sociological meanings by manipulating online documents. Sherry's lesson seemed to be that "what you think you see probably isn't what happened, because there is so much you don't know." That is a good lesson for any teacher or professor. I now wonder if the laughter was less about the students and more indicative of how vulnerable faculty feel when they enter the minefield of uncertainty underlying their own practice of an infinitely difficult craft.

Resources

Batson, Trent, and Bass, Randy. "Teaching and Learning in the Computer Age: Primacy of Process." *Change*, 1996, 28(2), 42–47.

Brown, John Seely. "Growing Up Digital: How the Web Changes Work, Education, and the Ways People Learn." *Change*, 2000, 32(2), 10–20.

Cambridge, Barbara (ed.). *Electronic Portfolios: Emerging Practices in Student, Faculty, and Institutional Learning.* Washington, D.C.: American Association for Higher Education, 2001.

Hall, Rogers. "Videorecording as Theory." In A. Kelly and Richard Lesh (eds.), *The Handbook of Research Design in Mathematics and Science Education.* Hillsdale, N.J.: Lawrence Erlbaum Associates, 2000.

Lesh, Richard, and Lehrer, Richard. "Iterative Refinement Cycles for Videotape Analyses of Conceptual Change." In A. Kelly and Richard Lesh (eds.), *The Handbook of Research Design in Mathematics and Science Education.* Hillsdale, N.J.: Lawrence Erlbaum Associates, 2000.

Pointer, Desiree. "Multimedia Tutorial for the Scholarship of Teaching." The Carnegie Foundation for the Advancement of Teaching. [http://kml.carnegiefoundation.org/tutorial]. 2000.

Internet Resources

The Carnegie Foundation Knowledge Media Laboratory (multimedia exhibits of work by scholars of teaching and learning, some including video). [http://www.carnegiefoundation.org/kml/]. N.d.

Third International Mathematics and Science Study—Repeat Video Study [http://nces.ed.gov/timss/timss-r/video.asp]. 1999.

Visible Knowledge Project. [http://crossroads.georgetown.edu/vkp/]. N.d.

Questions to Shape Practice

This volume attempts to convey both the difficulty of ethical issues in the scholarship of teaching and learning and the potential they hold, as we think them through and discuss them with colleagues, for prompting thought and reflection that can improve the quality of our work with students. In this spirit, the following twelve questions (generated through discussion with the case authors whose work appears in this volume, and with CASTL staff) are meant to foster awareness and discussion of ethical issues encountered in the scholarship of teaching and learning. The list is meant to be suggestive, not comprehensive or final. Please feel free to copy, adapt, and use it.

Purposes and Preparation

1. What is the question or problem you want to investigate, and why is it important enough to spend your own and others' time and energy on it?
2. What power relationships need to be taken into account in negotiating roles, permissions, and involvements by various participants in your work? Are there issues of gender, race, culture, and status difference that need especially to be taken into account?
3. What concerns might students have about your work and their participation in it? What choices do students have if they are uncomfortable?
4. Does your campus have an Institutional Review Board? What expectations exist about IRB review of projects in the scholarship of teaching and learning? If this is unfamiliar ground for you, where can you turn for information?

Methods

5. What methods will you use in your investigation? Whose consent, permission, cooperation, involvement, or collaboration will be required by these methods? What are the best ways to seek this consent, permission, etc., and at what point(s) in the work? How can roles and permissions be negotiated and renegotiated over time?
6. How can students be involved in your investigation? Might they play a role in gathering and analyzing data? How can the project be made educationally valuable for students?

Results and the Presentation of Results to Various Audiences

7. Whose perspectives will be represented in the work? How can various perspectives be honored? What special concerns do you have about representing individuals or groups who have less power in the educational system?

8. What negative or embarrassing data can you anticipate emerging from your scholarship of teaching and learning, and who might be harmed as a consequence? How can you create a context for understanding "bad news"? How, in particular, can examples of work by students who are novices, or who are struggling with new material, be treated with respect?

9. Who will see the results and products of your work? What conclusions might be drawn by various audiences: About students? About teaching? About your department, discipline or campus? About higher education? About you? How is your choice of medium (e.g., video) related to these concerns?

10. How can contributions to your work by various participants (including both colleagues and students) be acknowledged and/or cited, while maintaining confidentiality where appropriate?

Reflection and Development

11. Whom can you talk to about the above questions? How can you create occasions for discussion and reflection about them with colleagues?

12. What are you learning from your project that can inform future practice related to ethical issues in the scholarship of teaching and learning?

annotated BIBLIOGRAPHY

Research Ethics and the Scholarship of Teaching and Learning

James Bequette
Research Assistant
The Carnegie Foundation for the Advancement of Teaching
Chris Bjork
Education
Vassar College

This Annotated Bibliography was created to assist faculty with ethical questions that arise when investigating their teaching and their students' learning. Because there is little literature focused specifically on ethical issues in the scholarship of teaching and learning, the bibliography draws on a variety of fields, perspectives, and contexts. A number of themes run through the cited materials: unequal power relationships between scholars and the people they study; problematic aspects of representing research subjects in print and other media; the process of obtaining informed consent; the history of federal regulations for monitoring research; and "tales from the field" about dilemmas that scholars face as they attempt to apply ethical guidelines to actual research projects.

Anderson, P. V. "Simple Gifts: Ethical Issues in the Conduct of Person-Based Composition Research." CCC, 1998, 49(1), 63–93.
   This article attempts to deepen and broaden the discussion of issues related to person-based research. Anderson raises a series of questions likely to resonate with scholars of teaching and learning: Should disciplinary organizations develop guidelines to supplement IRB requirements? Can scholars disclose information about specific students that they have obtained outside formally planned research projects? Is there some way to balance our ethical obligations to future students with our ethical obligations to current and past students? He does not provide answers to such questions, or solutions to the dilemmas bound to face academics attempting to improve the quality of teaching and learning. Instead, he encourages researchers to "take collective responsibility for increasing awareness of and compliance with federal and institutional policies designed to protect the participants in formally planned research." Also included is an outline of federal and discipline-based regulations, beginning with the Nuremberg Code, that have been used to guide research practices in the United States.

Barnes, J. A. *The Ethics of Inquiry in Social Science*. Delhi: Oxford University Press, 1977.
   The text of this volume consists entirely of three lectures Barnes delivered at the Institute for Social and Economic Change in 1975: "Social Inquiry and Pluralist Society," "Ethical Problems in Practice," and "Social Science in a Post-Imperial World." The lectures provide a detailed picture of the development of standards related to research ethics during the twentieth century, with specific attention to major ethical dilemmas that have shaped the field of anthropology. Barnes does address the researcher-informant relationship, but focuses more on problematic aspects of government sponsorship of research projects.

———. *Who Should Know What? Social Science, Privacy, and Ethics*. Middlesex, England: Penguin Books, 1979.

> The concept of knowledge as power lies at the center of this discussion of the ethical problems that often arise in connection with social science research. Barnes frames social inquiry as a process of interaction and negotiation among "scientist, sponsor, gatekeeper, and citizens." Inherent differences in status and power between these groups makes research a potentially destructive undertaking. Any attempt to resolve the ethical issues related to such research must take into account the distribution of power among all parties involved. Barnes argues that negotiation will produce more appropriate responses to tensions among groups than will "the application of operationalized rules of procedure." Another interesting aspect of this book is the connection Barnes establishes between activity in the academic world and broader societal trends.

Bell, A. "FERPA—The Keys to Compliance." A Legal Memorandum. Reston, Va.: National Association of Secondary School Principals, 2001.

> This National Association of Secondary School Principals publication outlines the difficulty some schools have complying with the 1974 Family Educational Rights and Privacy Act (FERPA). Specifically, Bell, the association's associate legal counsel, explores the right to nondisclosure under this act, pertaining specifically to individual student records—report cards, documents, videos, computer media, grades and assessments—and the release of information to third parties.

Bloom, L. R. "Locked in 'Uneasy Sisterhood': Reflections on Feminist Methodology and Research Relations." *Anthropology & Education Quarterly*, 1997, 28(1), 111–122.

> In this piece, Bloom reflects upon a relationship that she shared with an informant who was participating in a project on life histories of feminist educators. More specifically, she describes a particular interaction that forced her to reexamine the feminist ideals that had guided her work up to that point. The event, and the subsequent self-scrutiny that it catalyzed, led Bloom to conclude that "feminist methodology's challenge to researchers to put themselves on the same critical plane as their research respondents is one of the most important practices of feminist methodology and certainly the most difficult to achieve." The author's honest questioning of her own practices makes this piece an interesting read as well as a model of the value of critical self-reflection by researchers.

"Bloomington Campus Committee for the Protection of Human Subjects: Students as Subjects." Indiana University Office of Research and University Graduate School. [http://www.Indiana.edu/~resrisk/stusub.html]. Aug. 2001.

> This committee report answers questions about whether a "researcher can use his/her own students as subjects." In general, the committee recommends that professors try to avoid using their own students as subjects in their research, claiming that such a policy "is in accord with that of other institutional review boards." However, using students in "research into teaching methods, curricula and other areas related to the scholarship of teaching and learning" is appropriate if "integral to the research." The report goes on to illustrate several models for doing so that "strike a balance" between the interests of teachers and students. For instance, the committee requires that the "student's written consent to use his or her own data, e.g., test results, papers written, homework, etc., be obtained after grades are entered." Also included are sample forms for getting this information both at the beginning of the semester and after grades are posted.

Burgess, R. G. (ed.). *The Ethics of Educational Research*. New York: The Falmer Press, 1989.

> This volume includes essays on a wide range of topics, from ethical issues in survey work to feminist research methodologies. A unifying theme is the fragile relationship between researcher and the individuals he or she studies; the way in which this relationship is negotiated will affect the collection, interpretation, and control of data. As one author comments, a daunting challenge to researchers is "balancing the

responsibilities to those who [are the focus of the research] against the need to present the findings in an uncompromising way to a wider audience." Although all of the essays are focused on research conducted in school settings, the issues raised should be of interest to higher education scholars of teaching and learning as well.

Campbell, P. W. "Ethics Panel Urges Better Safeguards for Human Research Subjects." *Chronicle of Higher Education*, Daily News, Dec. 10, 1998. [http://chronicle.com/daily/2002].
    Calling for the government to collect data on how Institutional Review Boards screen research proposals, Campbell discusses why an ethics panel called for Congress to "enact legislation requiring private organizations to adhere to the federal rules designed to protect human research subjects." Prepared by the Human Research Ethics Group—made up of scientists, lawyers, and sociologists—the panel report was part of the Project on Informed Consent at the Center for Bioethics at the University of Pennsylvania Health System. The article notes that the President's Advisory Committee on Human Radiation Experiments, the General Accounting Office, and the Inspector General for the Department of Health and Human Services recently arrived at similar conclusions.

Cassell, J. "Risk and Benefit to Subjects of Fieldwork." *The American Sociologist*, 1978, 13, 134–143.
    This article presents a set of comparisons between medical experimentation and social science fieldwork. According to Cassell, the most significant differences between the two types of research lie in the areas of power and control, direction of interaction, and scope of interaction. Cassell points out that most human-subjects regulations were drafted with a model of medical experimentation in mind, and may not be appropriate for fieldwork. She argues that subjects of fieldwork are at risk, but need a different type of protection than that developed with subjects of medical experiments in mind. Another topic included in this essay is risks and benefits associated with the publication of data.

———. "Ethical Principles for Conducting Fieldwork." *American Anthropologist*, 1980, 82, 28–41.
    Cassell reviews four "ideal typical forms of research," locating each along a continuum that includes four dimensions: relative power of the researchers, control of the research setting, control of the research context, and direction of research interaction. She concludes that biomedical experimentation and participant observation are located at opposite ends of the spectrum, with significant differences in calculable risks to participants. For this reason, it makes sense to evaluate the ethical appropriateness of ethnographic research in the context of respect for individual autonomy rather than on the basis of utilitarian risk-benefit estimates.

Cassell, J., and Jacobs, S. E. (eds.). *Handbook on Ethical Issues in Anthropology*. Washington, D.C.: American Anthropological Association, 1987.
    A collection of essays written by anthropologists who have served on the AAA Committee on Ethics, this book is grounded in the actual dilemmas that anthropologists face while working in the field. The first essay, by Murray Wax, provides a history of the development of ethics within the field of anthropology, beginning with the work of Franz Boas. Two of the chapters that follow present a series of "tales from the field" submitted to Jacobs and Cassell during their tenure as editors of the "Ethical Dilemmas" column in the *Anthropology Newsletter*, as well as commentary provided by readers in response. Other topics covered include techniques that encourage students to question research procedures, and a guide to organizing a workshop on ethical problems in fieldwork.

Charles, C. M. *Introduction to Educational Research*. New York: Longman, 1988.
    In this primer for conducting educational research, Charles distinguishes legal issues from ethical issues. In dealing with the latter, the author calls for beneficence, honesty, and accurate disclosure. Of note for the scholarship of teaching and learning is Charles's assessment that research conducted in educational settings, e.g., "classroom practices, methods of teaching, instructional strategies, and classroom management," is exempt by law from IRBs.

annotated bibliography

Christakis, N. A. "Should IRBs Monitor Research More Strictly?" *IRB*, 1988, 10(2), 8–10.

> Institutional Review Boards (IRBs) generally do a thorough job investigating a proposed research project prior to its commencement, according to Christakis, but they rarely monitor work in progress. This article considers the viability of extending the scope of IRBs to include some form of ongoing surveillance. Proponents of increased "policing" by IRBs argue that the current approach fails adequately to protect research subjects; critics point to the danger of compromising trust between researchers and IRBs. Christakis summarizes the key points made by each side of the argument without coming out strongly in favor of either approach.

Clark, C. T., and Moss, P. A. "Researching With: Ethical and Epistemological Implications of Doing Collaborative, Change-Oriented Research with Teachers and Students." *Teachers College Record*, 1996, 97(4), 518–548.

> The nature of the research project described in this paper adds an additional layer of complexity to the issues of informed consent and representation of subjects' views. Clark and Moss enlisted a group of high school students to interview their peers about literacy. The authors note that this approach is unique in that it "is not done 'on' or 'about' students and teachers; rather, it is done 'with' these groups." Although excerpts from student portfolios are included, Clark and Moss focus on ethical issues tied to gaining consent from participants more than on the use of writing samples. In another section, however, they note that the potential risks to subjects often derive more from publication of the findings than from the research process itself.

Denscombe, M., and Aubrook, L. "'It's Just Another Piece of Schoolwork': The Ethics of Questionnaire Research on Pupils in Schools." *British Educational Research Journal*, 1992, 18(2), 113–131.

> The authors discuss the ramifications of asking students to fill out questionnaires during class time. Denscombe and Aubrook assert that even when instructors tell students that participation in research projects is "optional," it is "assumed" that they will take part: "The subordinates might be informed and they might agree to cooperate, but such informed consent is not necessarily free from an element of coercion. It may not be entirely voluntary." When research is conducted in a school setting, "the context is inscribed by differential power relations."

Duster, T.; Matza, D.; and Wellman, D. "Field Work and the Protection of Human Subjects." *The American Sociologist*, 1979, 14(August), 136–142.

> This article provides an interesting contrast to most writing on research ethics and informed consent. The authors assert that the requirement to obtain informed consent is not advisable in all situations; in some instances it may actually impede the protection of human subjects. Research on unethical behavior, for example, would be difficult to conduct if research subjects were thoroughly briefed on the details of the project. For this reason, the "consequences of an inflexible administration of consent forms" need to be more seriously considered.

Emerson, R. M. (ed.). *Contemporary Field Research*. Boston: Little, Brown & Co., 1983.

> This collection of essays about development in theory and methodology related to social science fieldwork provides a comprehensive view of the researcher-informant relationship in the fields of sociology and anthropology. Of particular interest are the pieces by Van Maanen, Wax, and Galliher included in the final section, "Political and Ethical Implications in Field Research." The ideas articulated by Wax provide an interesting balance to more politically correct views published in recent years. The process of consent should remain flexible, he argues, and "cannot be formalized." Increasing controls on social science research will threaten the hard-fought freedoms earned by academics and may inhibit future research projects.

Faden, R. "Protecting Human Subjects." *Chronicle of Higher Education*, Oct. 20, 1995, p. A56.
   The author headed the Clinton-appointed Advisory Committee on Human Radiation Experiments and in this context studied human subjects protection from 1944 to 1974. But Faden's report of findings is more general, calling for additional "mechanisms to update interpretations of federal ethics rules as research advances" and "more oversight of the system regulating human research." Her committee called for more expedited review of nonproblematic proposals so those cases that risk real harm could be looked at more carefully.

Gadamer, H. G. *Truth and Method*. New York: Crossroad, 1975.
   Following the lead of Heidegger, Gadamer discusses the fundamental function of prejudices in any hermeneutical situation. Rather than obstacles to understanding, and thus needing correction or elimination, prejudices are for Gadamer "preunderstandings," prior, inescapable ways of knowing that belong to the interpreter's historical reality and to his or her being-in-the-world, which thus make his or her understanding possible. Gadamer's revision of the notion of prejudice, which the enlightenment had discredited, can have implications for the scholarship of teaching in so far as it demands that its practitioners consider, cogently and respectfully, the extent to which a student's acts of understanding constitute the subject matter of and for their investigations.

Galliher, J. F. "The ASA Code of Ethics on the Protection of Human Beings: Are Students Humans Too?" *The American Sociologist*, 1975, 10(May), 113–117.
   If research subjects are protected under the American Sociology Association Code of Ethics, Galliher contends, the same protection should be extended to students. Opening the instructional process up to review may be threatening to some faculty, but it will also raise important issues about the moral responsibilities of teachers of sociology. Galliher underlines the linkages between research and teaching and makes a case promoting a more synthetic conception of the role of the sociologist. Included in this article is a rationale for broadening the code, as well as a list of possible modifications.

Gose, B. "Privacy Law Does Not Preclude Use of Student Graders, Supreme Court Rules." *Chronicle of Higher Education*, Mar. 1, 2002, p. A25.
   In 2002, a 9-to-0 Supreme Court ruling reversed a lower court decision that peer grading violates the Family Educational Rights and Privacy Act (FERPA). The case stems from a lawsuit filed by the mother of a boy with special needs who was called a "dummy" by a peer "when his poor grades were read aloud to sixth-grade classmates," according to the author. In a related higher education case, the court will decide whether an individual has the right to sue a college for violating FERPA.

Graham, H. "Surveying Through Stories." In C. Bell and H. Roberts (eds.), *Social Researching: Politics, Problems, Practice*. London: Routledge & Kegan Paul, 1984.
   In this essay, Graham describes how and why she shifted from more traditional methodologies to a "surveying through stories" approach, and documents how the quality of the data generated was enriched as a result. The tendency for social science researchers to exploit and misrepresent the subjects they study (women, in particular) led Graham to search for alternative methods of data collection. Surveys and semistructured interviews "encourage respondents to reduce their experiences to fragments which can be captured in a question-and-answer format." Storytelling, in contrast, more effectively safeguards the rights of informants and provides them with opportunities to communicate the complexity of their experiences.

Hamilton, N. W. "Academic Freedom and Responsibility Symposium. Academic Tradition and the Principles of Professional Conduct." *Journal of College and University Law*, 2001, 609(Winter), 1–62.
   In this article from the National Association of College and University Attorneys, Hamilton worries that the loss of noncapitalist values and the triumph of a market mentality in the academic professions (and in law and medicine) has led to "the surrender of positive guild values—of collegiality, of concern

annotated BIBLIOGRAPHY

for the group, of a higher professional ethic beyond mere profit." He cites increased corporate financial support and possible conflict of interest in academic research as examples of lost autonomy in the learned professions. Increased interest in and development of codes of ethics and principles of conduct in scientific fields and some disciplinary societies outside the sciences are noted. "Some of the federal agencies, for example the National Institutes of Health, require that grant recipients provide formal training on research ethics" and some fields routinely require ethics courses for graduate students, according to the author. He references the American Association of University Professors' Statement of Professional Ethics and the Canadian Society for Teaching and Learning's definition of teaching that implies sound behavior: "content competence, pedagogical competence, valid assessment of students." (See also Murray, H., et al., "Ethical Principles for College and University Teaching." *New Directions for Teaching and Learning*, 1996, Summer, 57–62. Also see Braxton, J., and Bayer, A. *Faculty Misconduct in Collegiate Teaching*, 1999.)

Hammack, F. M. "Ethical Issues in Teacher Research." *Teachers College Record*, 1997, 99(2), 246–265.
Hammock examines issues surrounding teachers who conduct research in their own classrooms. He highlights the dilemmas that may stem from the dual teacher-researcher role. One of the strongest points he makes is that nontraditional research methodologies that aim to blur the distinction between researcher and practitioner may actually increase the potential for ethical problems to arise. Power differentials between instructor and student are also covered in depth. Although interested primarily in the work of classroom teachers, Hammock also refers to approaches taken by researchers working in other disciplines.

Helmers, M. H. *Writing Students: The Composition Testimonials and Representations of Students*. Albany, N.Y.: State University of New York Press, 1994.
This book is concerned with the characteristics of teachers' accounts of student writers rather than the ethical dimensions of using student work in research. Helmers raises important questions about the impact that discourse has on relations of power between teachers and students. Testimonials tend to depict writing students as individuals who lack skills and are expected to fail, but can be "corrected" by their instructors. This type of representation exaggerates the importance of teachers' actions and dismisses the efforts of student writers. Helmers underlines the need to reconsider the way in which scholars interact with and depict their students.

Howe, K. R., and Dougherty, K. C. "Ethics, Institutional Review Boards, and the Changing Face of Educational Research." *Educational Researcher*, 1993, December, 16–21.
Howe and Dougherty begin with a history of IRBs and the rationale behind exemptions that were granted to academics investigating teaching and learning processes. They debate whether IRBs or specialists within disciplines are best prepared to make judgments about the appropriateness of research practices. The original justification for granting educational researchers exemptions needs to be re-examined, they contend, due to substantial increases in the volume of qualitative research conducted in academic institutions. Qualitative and experimental methodologies often foster close relationships between researchers and subjects or participants, and therefore require careful scrutiny in the area of ethics.

Kahn, J. P., and Mastroianni, A. C. "Doing Research Well by Doing Right." *Chronicle of Higher Education*, Feb. 15, 2002, p. B24.
In light of controversy surrounding the death of participants in medical studies and exploitation of children of low social and economic status in others, the authors report that compliance oversight is important but "recognizing the ethical commitments at the core of research" is key. A question is raised: "How can institutions and researchers move away from the culture of compliance," and toward "a culture of conscience?" The authors answer this question by proposing that subjects, institutions, and researchers operate as partners (albeit unequal partners) through all phases of the research process.

"Subjects can never be equal partners with researchers, because researchers are the ones who develop the studies and choose the subjects." However, subjects must be more proactive when considering their role and the risks associated with participation. Ethics and sound clinical practice are synonymous, according to Kahn and Mastroianni, and "institutions must work to change their cultures." Suggestions for doing so include requiring researchers to take ethics courses and engage in open and ongoing communication with colleagues about ethical issues.

Kiernan, V. "Use of 'Cookies' in Research Sparks a Debate Over Privacy." *Chronicle of Higher Education*, Sept. 25, 1998, p. A31.

Using "cookies," small computer files that track Web users' online behavior, has raised the ire of critics in academe who view this type of research as unethical. The issue of "informed consent" is raised by researchers who claim that online users should be notified before they become part of even the most benign research projects, while others assume a pro-technology perspective and argue that an "implied consent" approach is ethical as long as Web users are assured anonymity. The article cites projects at the University of Wisconsin–Madison and at the University of Washington.

Kirsch, G. E. *Ethical Dilemmas in Feminist Research*. Albany, N.Y.: State University of New York Press, 1999.

Kirsch focuses on the politics of location, representation, and publication. Her discussions of the dilemmas that confront feminist researchers as they attempt to capture and write about the experiences of others are highly relevant to scholars of teaching and learning. Among the issues she addresses are the multiple roles and competing tasks demanded of researchers working in institutional settings, the nature of informed consent and the limitations of IRBs in addressing the realities of qualitative research, and tensions that arise when the scene of inquiry is also a scene of evaluation. Kirsch recognizes that facing such challenges can "seem overwhelming, even paralyzing," but stresses that dialogue centered on ethical issues can also be "enabling and generative."

Lincoln, Y. S. "Toward a Categorical Imperative for Qualitative Research." In E. Eisner and A. Peshkin (eds.), *Qualitative Inquiry in Education*. New York: Teachers College Press, 1990.

This piece is a response to two other papers included in the volume, which Lincoln uses as a springboard for a discussion of broader issues and themes tied to changes in the landscape of qualitative research practices. The shift from the logical positivist to phenomenological systems, she asserts, requires a reconceptualization of the ethical principles that guide qualitative research. Given that research participants are now viewed differently, new rules addressing the relationship between researcher and researched need to be developed. Toward the end of the essay, Lincoln offers a set of principles, based on Kantian philosophy, that attempt to define "what constitutes ethical behavior in a revisionist and revolutionary research world."

Mortensen, P., and Kirsch, G. E. (eds.). *Ethics and Representation in Qualitative Studies of Literacy*. Urbana, Ill.: National Council of Teachers of English, 1996.

The editors describe this volume not as a "handbook" of qualitative research methods but rather as "a book that illuminates the complex ethical and representational questions that are rarely discussed in research manuals." Many of its essays are cited in the introduction to this volume.

Phillips, S. R. "Asking the Sensitive Question: The Ethics of Survey Research and Teen Sex." *IRB*, 1994, 16(6), 1–6.

In this piece, Phillips argues that the requirements tied to IRBs often do not provide an adequate "safety net" for many research projects. Simply following the rules is "insufficient to assure quality, ethical research." Phillips does not, however, advocate more stringent regulation of research activities. Instead, she advises researchers to rely on their own notions of morality and ethical behavior. The bulk of this article details the specific strategies Phillips used to ensure that the high school students she surveyed for a study on adolescent sexual behavior were protected. These descriptions evidence a painstaking effort by the author to consider the implications of every decision she made in conjunction with survey design and administration.

Pritchard, I. A. "Travelers and Trolls: Practitioner Research and Institutional Review Boards." *Educational Researcher*, 2002, 31(3), 3–13.
Pritchard examines the conflicts and misunderstandings that sometimes plague relationships between practitioner researchers (including scholars of teaching and learning but also scholars in other practice-oriented settings) and Institutional Review Boards. Some difficulties stem from different conceptions of *research*—a term that "practitioner researchers apply … more widely than IRBs." Other difficulties follow from the characteristics of practitioner research, for instance the relationship between researchers and subjects. Pritchard also looks at circumstances that complicate the work of IRBs, including work overload, unfamiliarity with practitioner research, and inflexible regulations. The article ends with suggestions for improving relationships between practitioner researchers and IRBs.

Protecting Human Beings: Institutional Review Boards and Social Science Research. Washington, D.C.: American Association of University Professors, 2001.
This draft report prepared by the AAUP considers the experiences of scholars and social scientists in disciplines governed by rules protecting human subjects. Representatives from the American Anthropological Association, the American Historical Association, the American Political Science Association, the American Sociological Association, the Oral History Association, and the Organization of American Historians convened in November 1999 and May 2000. Four areas outlined in their report are government regulations; IRBs and the notion of academic freedom; "the Common Rule," or federal policy on human-subject research; and recommendations for improvement of IRB practices. The report can be found online at: http://www.aaup.org/statements/Redbook/repirb.htm.

Zeni, J. (ed). *Ethical Issues in Practitioner Research*. New York: Teachers College Press, 2001.
In her foreword, Susan Lytle calls this the "first full-length volume devoted to ethical issues" in practitioner research on teaching and learning. More specifically, the various chapters focus on insider investigation of teaching and learning emerging from the inquiry of both K–12 teachers and university-based practitioners. Zeni posits that educational reform has helped kindle a newfound interest in practitioner research yet notes that many people with little "grounding in either research methods or ethical safeguards" are now conducting inquiry in schools. Moreover, ethical guidelines, when they exist, usually ignore or are inappropriate in the situation of the insider. "As a result they miss the ethical dilemmas most often encountered by teachers studying their own classrooms," says Zeni, which tend to be "ambiguous, context-sensitive, and therefore resistant to generic regulations." In response, the author provides a guide to ethical decision making for insider research in her epilogue to this volume.

Internet Resources

Ethics Information from Professional Associations

http://www.aaanet.org/committees/ethics/ethcode.htm
American Anthropological Association

http://www.aera.net/about/policy/ethics.htm
American Educational Research Association

http://www.lsadc.org/humsubjs.html
Linguistic Society of America

http://www.apa.org/ethics/code.html
   American Psychological Association

http://www.archaeological.org/About_the_AIA/ethics.html
   Archaeological Institute of America

http://www.asanet.org/ecoderev.htm
   American Sociological Association

http://www.rpanet.org/
   Register of Professional Archeologists

http://www.sfaa.net/sfaaethic.html
   Society for Applied Anthropology

Other Relevant Sites

http://humansubjects.stanford.edu/nonmedical/
   The Web site for the Stanford University Administrative Panel on Human Subjects in Nonmedical Research. Includes a set of guidelines for obtaining informed consent.

http://kerlins.net/bobbi/research/qualresearch/consentletter.html
   A sample letter of informed consent posted on the Internet.

http://nexus.sscl.uwo.ca/anthropology/jorgensen/ethics_pages.htm
   A comprehensive directory of all ethics statements posted on the Web by various anthropology associations around the world.

http://ohrp.osophs.dhhs.gov/
   The Office for Human Research Protections. Includes links to human subjects–related news, grant application forms that can be downloaded, information on research training opportunities, and career resources.

http://ohrp.osophs.dhhs.gov/irb/irb_guidebook.htm
   Information about the IRB 1993 Guidebook designed to assist Institutional Review Board (IRB) members, researchers, and institutional administrators in fulfilling their responsibilities for protecting the rights and welfare of human subjects.

http://www.access.gpo.gov/nara/cfr/index.html
   The Code of Regulations page for the National Archives and Records Office. Use the browser to find the specific regulations that interest you.

http://www.cis.yale.edu/grants/policies.html
   The Yale University Office of Grant and Contract Administration homepage. Includes sections on federal regulations, university guidelines, and informed consent forms.

http://www.ed.gov/offices/OCFO/humansub.html
   Homepage for the U.S. Department of Education, Protection of Human Subjects in Research.

BIOGRAPHICAL notes

James Bequette is a doctoral student at Stanford University and a former K–12 and community-college art and journalism teacher. In working on his dissertation, he has grappled with ethical concerns surrounding ethnographic research at a predominantly American Indian school and what role non-native art educators play in connecting children with their cultural heritage. He is a research assistant at The Carnegie Foundation for the Advancement of Teaching.

Chris Bjork is a member of the Education Department at Vassar College. His research interests center on educational reform and school contexts that promote instructional excellence. While a graduate student, he served as a research assistant at the Carnegie Foundation, where he worked on the annotated bibliography that appears in this volume. Previously, he worked as a classroom teacher in both the United States and Asia.

Pat Hutchings is a vice president of The Carnegie Foundation for the Advancement of Teaching, where she and Lee S. Shulman direct the Carnegie Academy for the Scholarship of Teaching and Learning (CASTL). Hutchings has written and spoken widely about the investigation and documentation of teaching and learning.

Lee S. Shulman has been president of The Carnegie Foundation for the Advancement of Teaching since 1997. Shulman's scholarship has focused on the improvement of teaching in K–12 and university settings, on new approaches to the assessment of teaching, and on the methods and quality of education research. Shulman is former president of the American Educational Research Association and past president of the National Academy of Education.